100 WAL...
Norfolk

compiled by

Chris Chorley
Bill Pywell
Bobbie Sauerzapf
&
James Saunders

The Crowood Press

First published in 1997 by
The Crowood Press Ltd
Ramsbury
Marlborough
Wiltshire SN8 2HR

British Library Cataloguing-in-Publication Data
A catalogue record for this book is
available from the British Library

ISBN 1 86126 016 4

All maps by Janet Powell

Typeset by Carreg Limited, Ross-on-Wye, Herefordshire

Printed by J. W. Arrowsmith Limited, Bristol

CONTENTS

35.	Wymondham	5m	(8km)
36.	Narborough and Marham Fen	5m	(8km)
37.	Fring	5m	(8km)
38.	Bawsey and Leziate	5m	(8km)
39.	Brancaster	5m	(8km)
40.	Snettisham	5m	(8km)
41.	... and longer version	10m	(16km)
42.	Syderstone	5m	(8km)
43.	... and longer version	8m	(13km)
44.	Bircham	5m	(8km)
45.	Swaffham	$5\frac{1}{4}$m	($8\frac{1}{2}$km)
46.	Belaugh	$5\frac{1}{2}$m	(9km)
47.	How Hill	$5\frac{1}{2}$m	(9km)
48.	Bressingham	$5\frac{1}{2}$m	($8\frac{1}{4}$km)
49.	Lyng	$5\frac{1}{2}$m	(9km)
50.	North Creake	$5\frac{1}{2}$m	(9km)
51.	Banham	$5\frac{3}{4}$m	(9km)
52.	Mannington Hall	6m	($9\frac{1}{2}$km)
53.	... and longer version	$9\frac{1}{2}$m	(15km)
54.	Trunch	6m	($9\frac{1}{2}$km)
55.	Horsford	6m	($9\frac{1}{2}$km)
56.	Dilham and Honing	6m	($9\frac{1}{2}$km)
57.	Knapton	6m	($9\frac{1}{2}$km)
58.	Happisburgh	6m	($9\frac{1}{2}$km)
59.	Trowse and Kirby Bedon	6m	($9\frac{1}{2}$km)
60.	Middleton Towers and East Winch	6m	(10km)
61.	Coltishall Green	$6\frac{1}{2}$m	($10\frac{1}{2}$km)
62.	Aldborough	$6\frac{1}{2}$m	($10\frac{1}{2}$km)
63.	Intwood	$6\frac{1}{2}$m	($10\frac{1}{2}$km)
64.	Barnham Broom	$6\frac{1}{2}$m	($10\frac{1}{2}$km)
65.	Pulham Market and Pulham St Mary	$6\frac{1}{2}$m	($10\frac{1}{2}$km)
66.	Walsingham	$6\frac{1}{4}$m	(10km)
67.	Northrepps	7m	(11km)
68.	Reepham, Salle and Heydon	7m	(11km)
69.	... and longer version	11m	($17\frac{1}{2}$km)
70.	Worstead	7m	(11km)

71.	Claxton	7m	(11km)
72.	Mattishall	7m	(11km)
73.	Salhouse	7m	(11km)
74.	Mundham and Sisland	7m	(11km)
75.	Martham and West Somerton	7m	(11km)
76.	Wells-next-the-Sea and Warham	7m	(11km)
77.	The Great Eastern Pingo Trail	7m	(11km)
78.	Gressenhall	7m	(11km)
79.	Tittleshall and Mileham	7m	(11km)
80.	Reepham	$7^1/_2$m	(12km)
81.	Strumpshaw and Lingwood	$7^1/_2$m	(12km)
82.	Crostwick and Frettenham	$7^1/_2$m	(12km)
83.	Hethersett	$7^1/_2$m	(12km)
84.	Bale and Hindringham	$7^1/_2$m	(12km)
85.	Harpley Dams	$7^1/_2$m	(12km)
86.	Blickling Hall and Bure Valley	8m	(13km)
87.	Honingham	8m	(13km)
88.	Holt and Sheringham	8m	(13km)
89.	Loddon	8m	(15km)
90.	Long Stratton	8m	(13km)
91.	Castle Acre and West Acre	8m	(13km)
92.	Brooke	$8^1/_2$m	($13^1/_2$km)
93.	Blakeney and Glandford	$8^1/_2$m	($13^1/_2$km)
94.	Holkham and Burnham Overy	9m	($14^1/_2$km)
95.	Salthouse and Cley	10m	(16km)
96.	Shouldham Warren	10m	(16km)
97.	Ringstead and Holme-next-the-Sea	10m	(16km)
98.	Sheringham	$10^1/_2$m	(17km)
99.	Aylsham	11m	($17^1/_2$km)
100.	Burgh Castle and Belton	11m	($17^1/_2$km)

PUBLISHER'S NOTE

We very much hope that you enjoy the routes presented in this book, which has been compiled with the aim of allowing you to explore the area in the best possible way - on foot.

We strongly recommend that you take the relevant map for the area, and for this reason we list the appropriate Ordnance Survey maps for each route. Whilst the details and descriptions given for each walk were accurate at time of writing, the countryside is constantly changing, and a map will be essential if, for any reason, you are unable to follow the given route. It is good practice to carry a map and use it so that you are always aware of your exact location.

We cannot be held responsible if some of the details in the route descriptions are found to be inaccurate, but should be grateful if walkers would advise us of any major alterations. Please note that whenever you are walking in the countryside you are on somebody else's land, and we must stress that you should *always* keep to established rights of way, and *never* cross fences, hedges or other boundaries unless there is a clear crossing point.

Remember the country code:

Enjoy the country and respect its life and work
Guard against all risk of fire
Fasten all gates
Keep dogs under close control
Keep to public footpaths across all farmland
Use gates and stiles to cross field boundaries
Leave all livestock, machinery and crops alone
Take your litter home
Help to keep all water clean
Protect wildlife, plants and trees
Make no unnecessary noise

The walks are listed by length - from approximately 3 to 12 miles - but the amount of time taken will depend on the fitness of the walkers and the time spent exploring any points of interest along the way. Nearly all the walks are circular and most offer recommendations for refreshments.

Good walking.

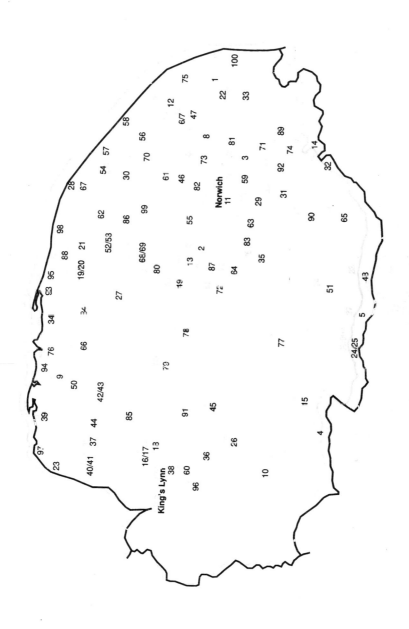

Norwich

King's Lynn

Maps: OS Sheets Landranger 134; Pathfinder 884.
A short parish walk offering typical Broadland views.
Start: At 462136, the Filby Bridge car park on the A1064, the
Acle to Caister road.

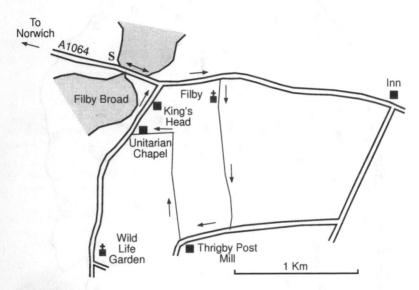

The car park is on the Norwich side of the Bridge: leave it at the corner nearest
Filby, following a short boardwalk, waymarked by yellow arrows, that avoids
walking along the road. Cross a wooden bridge and follow the main road (the
A1064), with care, through **Filby** for 1000 yards. Now turn right into Church Lane,
signposted 'To Church'. At the lane's end, enter the churchyard (dogs on leads
please), passing the church on your left and, just after a low wall which divides the
churchyard, turn left to reach a kissing gate. Go through and turn right along a
concrete bridleway.

Just after passing a large barn on your left, continue ahead up a headland strip
between fields, continuing later with a hedge on your left to reach a minor road.
Turn right along the road for 300 yards, then, just as the road swings sharp left, turn

right along a footpath indicated by a finger post and blue arrow. A short diversion from here – just around the corner – is **Thrigby Post Mill**: sorry, it has no sails!

Follow the footpath uphill between two fields, then walk with a hedge on your right. About 400 yards beyond the crest of a rise, turn left at a path junction and cross a small field along a well-marked path. Continue ahead with an orchard on your right, swinging around the far corner of the orchard to reach a **Unitarian Chapel** heritage site. Go through the site to reach a road. The walk turns right here: turning left takes you to the Thrigby Hall wildlife garden with its bird and animal collection, about $^3/_4$ mile down the road.

On reaching the main road, turn left and retrace your steps to Filby Broad car park. Twitchers may care to follow the short boardwalk from the far side of the car park to a bird hide overlooking the Broad: it is about 300 yards to the hide.

POINTS OF INTEREST:
Filby – The village name is derived from the Danish *fiel* meaning a board or plank. It is thought that the Norse chieftain's house here was built from planks rather than the usual log and mud. The suffix '-by' means a settlement. This part of the county was colonised by the Norsemen.
Thrigby Mill – The mill dates from 1790 and was used to grind corn.
Unitarian Chapel – The chapel was built in the 18th century but little now remains.

The walk covers a part of the county known, geologically, as 'Flegg', one of the most fertile parts of Norfolk.

REFRESHMENTS:
There are numerous possibilities in Filby. At the restaurant and café on the main road on the Filby side of the Bridge, the swans demands cake with menaces. The astute accede, the rest may like to don protective clothing.

Maps: OS Sheets Landranger 133; Pathfinder 882.

A tranquil riverside stroll.

Start: At 141137, the parking area opposite the Swan Inn, Ringland.

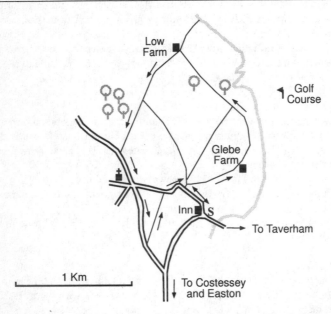

The Swan Inn, and the parking area, lie close to the **bridge** over the Wensum.

From the car park, head up 'The Street', and as the road bends left, and just after Chestnut Cottage and River View on your right, turn right up a track. Follow the track as it swings right and then left, ignoring a track off to your left.

    Go pass Glebe Farm, on your right, continuing along the track to pass a cattle pound, also on your right. Go through two gates (or over two stiles), then ignore a footpath off to your left to reach the end of the track at a field gate. Go through the gate (or over the stile) and follow the hedge on the left to reach a house set in the middle of the fields. At the end of the hedge, turn left through a gate and head for the gravel drive leading to the house. Turn away from house and follow the drive up and over a hill, passing a wood on your right. Ignore the path going left at the start of the wood, continuing along the drive to a minor road.

Turn left along the road to reach a T-junction by a **church**. Take the road opposite (signposted for Easton and Costessey), following it for 600 yards to reach a signed footpath on the left. Follow the path across a field, aiming for the point on its opposite side where the hedge you are walking towards meets a hedge at right angles. Go through a gap in the hedge and walk towards Ringland village, keeping a hedge on your right. Go through a gap in the hedge to reach 'The Street' and turn right along it to return to the start.

POINTS OF INTEREST:
Bridge – The bridge area is a favourite of local kids who spend long, hot summer days swimming, paddling and fishing here. If you indulge in such pastimes, please wash your feet first for the Wensum is a major source of drinking water for the city of Norwich!
St Peter's Church – The church is worth a look for its fine hammerbeam roof.

REFRESHMENTS:
The Swan Inn, Ringland.

Walk 3   **SURLINGHAM**   3m (5km)

Maps: OS Sheets Landranger 134; Pathfinder 903.

A riverside walk along typical Broadland reed and carr. One for the bird watchers.

Start: At 305065, Surlingham Church.

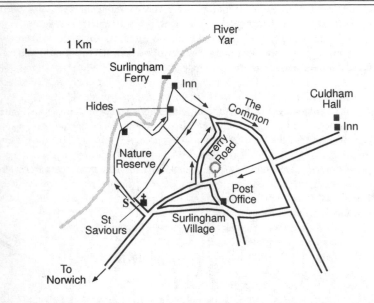

From the church, head downhill along an enclosed footpath, with a house on your right. Keep to the main path as it meets the River Yare and turns right. Keep dogs on leads here as there is a **Nature Reserve** immediately to your right. Keep small children on leads too (!) as the water is perilously close. Bird watchers may care to divert to the public hides on this stretch: these are provided to give good views into the reed beds of the Reserve.

At the end of the Reserve, continue ahead over a wooden bridge and dyke towards Surlingham's Ferry House Inn. Cross a stile into a garden and bear half-right to meet the tarmac drive to the inn. Turn right and walk uphill to a road. Turn left (signposted Coldham Hall).

Just after The Common becomes The Street, turn right up an enclosed footpath opposite 'Treetops'. Pass allotments on your right and continue uphill on a clear path along the right edge of two fields and copse to reach a minor road.

Maintain direction along the road to reach a fork. Turn right, downhill (signposted Surlingham Ferry/Ferry Road) and, where the road bends sharp right, about 700 yards after the fork, turn left down a drive signposted for Surlingham Ferry.

About 150 yards further on, turn left, just before 'Willow Cottage', and follow a footpath with the Nature Reserve on your right. After 400 yards, cross a stile on the right and continue in your original direction, now with a wire fence on your left. Ignore a footpath off to the right and continue to the Gun Club. Keep to the path here if firing is in progress. Go through a gate, then immediately turn left over a stile into a field. Cross the field on a clear path heading towards **Surlingham Church** on the skyline. Pass the ruins of **St Saviour's Church** and leave the field through a gate into a gravel track. Continue uphill to reach the church and the start.

POINTS OF INTEREST:

Surlingham Church Marsh Nature Reserve – The Reserve is owned and managed by the RSPB. Many wetland birds can be viewed here including the rare bittern, and hen harriers during the winter. The Reserve illustrates the natural progression from open water to reed bed. As leaves and silt clog the reed beds, alder and willow trees become established which hasten the silting and drying process.

The River Yare here is busy with all manner of waterborne traffic. You may see anything from a rowing eight to a luxury motor cruiser.

Surlingham Church – The church has a round Norman Tower with a later octagonal addition.

St Saviour's Church – The renowned naturalist A E (Ted) Ellis is buried in the ruins of St Saviour's. The family home, and the nature reserve he founded, are just down the road at Wheatfen.

REFRESHMENTS:
The Ferry House Inn, Surlingham.

Walk 4   WEETING   3m (4½km)

Maps: OS Sheets Landranger 144; Pathfinder 942.

A fine walk in Breckland, with a small village, woods and arable land.

Start: At 777892, Weeting Church.

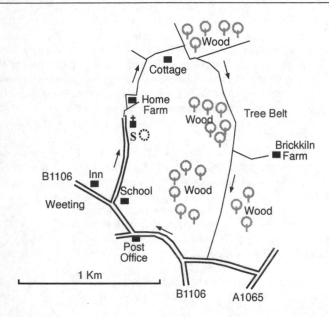

Start to the left of the church, going up a track and passing the farmhouse of Home Farm on the right. Go between the buildings and turn right at a waymarker. Turn left to leave the farmyard, with a pig shed on your right, and continue between fields, heading towards a cottage. At a track junction, turn right and go past the cottage, on your right, as you head towards a wood.

At a T-junction before the wood, turn right to follow a track leftwards around the wood. Shortly after the corner of the wood, bear right and walk with a field on your left to reach an ash plantation on the right, and a belt of trees on the left.

The track follows a southerly direction past the plantation. Ignore a track on the left to Brickkiln Farm, and continue across an open area with birch woods on your right. Follow the track between the birch trees to reach a minor road. Turn right to reach the road's junction with the B1106. Cross, with care, and turn right into Weeting. Before the bridge, cross the road and continue around the corner to reach the Green. Bear right to pass school and follow signs to the **castle** to return to the **church**.

POINTS OF INTEREST:

Castle – The castle was built in the late 12th century and is more a fortified manor house than a war engine. The remains of walls and part of the three-storey keep/ tower remain inside an unusual rectangular moat. The site is in the care of English Heritage and is open at any reasonable time.

St Mary's Church – The church has a round tower, which was rebuilt in the 19th century, and some fine old bench ends decorated with poppy heads.

REFRESHMENTS:

The Saxon Inn, Weeting.

Walk 5   **GARBOLDISHAM**   3$\frac{1}{2}$m (5$\frac{1}{2}$km)

Maps: OS Sheets 144; Pathfinder 943 and 944.

On the edge of Breckland: a typical village, conifer woods,
pasture and arable land.

Start: At 006816, the Fox Inn, Garboldisham.

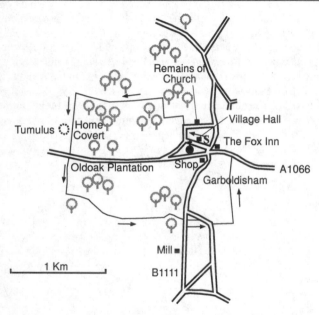

Off road parking is available opposite the Fox Inn or at the Village Hall car park.

From the Fox Inn, walk towards the **Church**, passing the Village Hall on your right.
Turn right into Back Street. The ruined church can be seen on your right. Now turn
left opposite a thatched cottage with stone acorns on the gateposts, going along the
side of a field and heading towards a wood and an electricity pole. Turn right beside
the wood (walking with the wood on your left) and, at its end, turn left to go along
the left edge of a field, still with the wood on your left. Go past a small clump of
trees on the right and go straight on along a track towards a wood. Continue with the
wood (Home Covert) on your left. Turn left at the wood's end, still walking with

woodland on your left. Note the tumulus on your right at this point – some of the tumuli (barrows) in the area are 90 feet in diameter and 18 feet high. Go through double gates to reach a road (the A1066).

Cross the road, with care, and go through a barrier. Continue down the track on the left, turning left before the gate at the end of the tree belt to go along the right edge of a field, with a fence on your right. Continue along the right edge of a large field (still with the fence on your right) for approximately $\frac{1}{2}$ mile to reach the corner of a wood. You will see a house on the left in the trees. Enter the wood along a narrow path, passing the house on your left to join a track leading to it. Turn right along this track to reach a road (the B1111). Cross the road, with care, and climb a stile into a sports field. Cross the field – you can see Garboldisham Mill on your right – to reach a minor road at the far left corner. Turn right and walk up the road and, just past bungalow on your right (Glenrosa), turn left along a signed track, following it – past farm buildings and, later, fields on your left – towards Garboldisham. The church and ruin passed at the start of the walk can be seen on the left. When a road (the A1066 again) is reached, turn left, with care, along the verge towards the Fox Inn. Just before completing the walk you will see the **village sign** across the road from the Fox Inn.

POINTS OF INTEREST:
Church – Dedicated to St John the Baptist the church dates from the early 14th century. The west tower has a chequered pattern of knapped flint and stone.
The ruins are those of All Saints' Church. The church tower is still standing.
Village Sign – This has a model of the Old Mill at the top and carvings symbolising the agricultural history of the area on the post. The Old Mill was a post mill, but it no longer functions.

REFRESHMENTS:
The Fox Inn, Garboldisham.

Walks 6 & 7   LUDHAM AND ST BENET'S ABBEY $3\frac{1}{2}$m ($5\frac{1}{2}$km) or 8m (13km)

Maps: OS Sheets Landranger 134; Pathfinder 883 and 884.
Broadland - past, present and future.
Start: At 392182, the car park in Horsefen Road, Ludham.

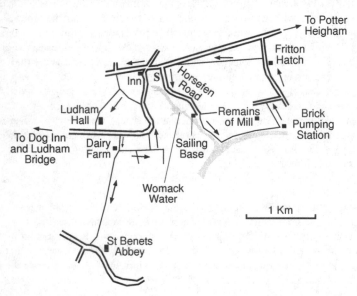

From the car park – reached by following the signs for the County School Sailing Base – turn right along the road, following it to the School Sailing Base. Take the footpath to the left of the Base (with Womack Water on your right), following it along the riverbank. When the path turns left the water on your right is the River Thurne. Continue along the riverbank until the path ends at a brick pumping station. There, turn left, away from river, and go over a wooden bridge. At a gravel track, turn left and continue to a T-junction. Turn right and walk to a road. Turn left. Opposite 'Fritton Hatch', on your right, turn left along a bridleway, walking with a hedge on your right. The bridleway becomes an enclosed green lane: follow this to a road. Turn left.

The shorter walk now turns left again to return to the start.

The longer route continues ahead, following the road through the village, passing the church and village hall on the left. About 500 yards after the church, turn left along a bridleway. When a fork is reached, take the right branch, passing Ludham Hall on your left. Continue down a farm drive to a road. Turn left, then take the next right turn down a concrete drive (there is a small green sign for St Benet's Abbey). Go past a dairy farm, on your right, and follow the drive for just over a mile to the ruins of **St Benet's Abbey**. Retrace your steps back to the dairy farm. Now, as the concrete drive bends right, turn right along a footpath which follows the right edge of a field. After 500 yards, at the end of the second field, turn left up a track to a road. Turn right to reach a T-junction. Turn left and follow the road to Ludham village, where there is an interesting mix of architecture. Turn right at the church, then take the next right to return to the start.

POINTS OF INTEREST:
St Benet's Abbey – The Abbey was founded by King Canute. It was taken by the Danes only after the treacherous actions of one monk. He was rewarded for his perfidy by being hanged in the gateway.

The landscape traversed by this route is man-made. You may care to ponder on these words from David Dymond's book *Norfolk Landscape* – 'Here more than anywhere else in Norfolk, we can see the awesome responsibilities placed on our generation. The competing claims of agriculture, leisure and sport must be heard, but, at the same time, the fragile ecological fabric which is infinitely more precious than any short term economic gain has to be maintained for posterity.'

Early in the walk you pass the remains of an old windpump used to drain the marshes, together with its modern, electric equivalent. Away to your right is a high-tech wind farm.

The Mill ruins passed early in the walks were, when fully functional, used to grind oil-seeds to provide lamp oil.

REFRESHMENTS:
There are several possibilities in Ludham.

Walk 8   **RANWORTH**   3$\frac{1}{2}$m (5$\frac{1}{2}$km)

Maps: OS Sheets Landranger 134; Pathfinder 883.

A delightful Broadland village and a chance to visit a Nature Reserve.

Start: At 360146, the Conservation Centre car park, Ranworth.

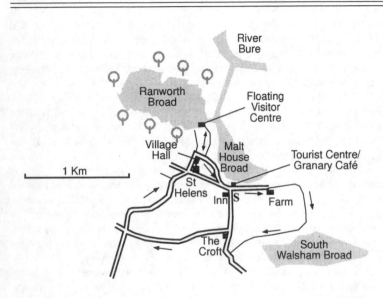

The car park is opposite the Maltsters Inn at Ranworth.

From car park, turn right along the road, walking away from the inn and the Visitor's Centre. Pass a thatched farm on your right, and continue ahead along a gravel track. The track later bends right, then right again, with a carr on your left: follow it past houses, on your right, to reach a road near the Anglian Water station.

Turn right, uphill, then, just after The Croft on your left, take the first road to the left. Follow the road to a crossroads at its end. Turn right and walk to another crossroads near the **church**. Go straight over and continue downhill.

Follow the road as it bends right at the Village Hall, then, after a further 200 yards, turn left into the Nature Reserve and follow the boardwalk to the Floating Visitor's Centre at **Ranworth and Malthouse Broads**. From there, retrace your steps to the road and turn left along it to reach a T-junction. Now turn left to return to start.

POINTS OF INTEREST:
Ranworth and Malthouse Broads – King George VI used to go wildfowling here as the guest of the Cator family. In 1949 Colonel Cator gave the Broads to the Norfolk Naturalists Trust as a reserve. A full explanation of the history and biology of Broadland is to be found in the Floating Visitor Centre. Until the 1950s it was thought that the Broads were a natural feature, as local history had been lost in the mists of time. It is now known that since Roman times peat had been dug here as the lack of trees led to a fuel shortage. Medieval monks turned the digging into a major industry to supply the growing city of Norwich and, most importantly, their monasteries. In the 14th century, a rise in the sea level caused flooding of the workings, leaving the shallow lakes seen today. Some, but not all, are linked directly to the area's rivers. All are liable to silting unless actively dredged. The Visitor's Centre fully explains the process known to ecologists as 'succession', where habitats and the creatures dwelling in them change with time. Eventually a stable community develops which is ideally suited to the climate and soil. In this part of Britain this 'climax' community is oak woodland.
St Helen's Church – The church may be open with a chance to climb the tower for a spectacular view of the Broads.

REFRESHMENTS:
The Maltsters Inn, Ranworth, at the start of the walk.
There is a café/restaurant opposite the car park, adjacent to the Tourist Information Centre.

Walk 9   **BURNHAM THORPE** $3^1/_2$m $(5^1/_2$km)

Maps: OS Sheets Landranger 132; Pathfinder 819.

Pleasant tracks around Nelson's birthplace.

Start: At 852416, The Green, adjacent to The Nelson Inn, Burnham Thorpe.

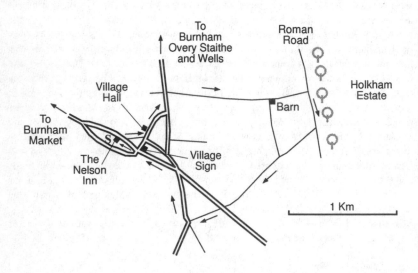

With your back to the inn, cross a playing field heading diagonally right to reach the Village Hall. Pass the hall on your left, then turn left, uphill, along a minor road to reach a T-junction. Turn left along a road signposted for Burnham Overy Staithe, but, after about 200 yards, turn right along a gravel track.

Follow the track for just under a mile, passing a barn, on the right, to reach a wall of the **Holkham Estate** and a wood. There, turn right along a signed footpath to reach, after 300 yards, a fork. Take the right branch, following the path, with trees on your left, for $^3/_4$ mile (south-westwards) to reach a road.

Cross the road and follow the track opposite to reach a minor road. Turn right to reach a crossroads. Now turn left to return to the start, passing the **village sign** along the way.

POINTS OF INTEREST:

Holkham Estate – The estate is the home of the Earls of Leicester. The grounds are open for public walking. The house is open too, but with restricted hours and only during the summer.

Village Sign – Burnham Thorpe was the birthplace of Admiral Lord Nelson – as recorded on the village sign. The Rectory where Nelson was born is no more, but the more modern building on the site is marked by a plaque. Ask in the village if you wish to hunt out the spot. The little stream through the village is the River Burn. It was formerly navigable to a point just above the present village.

There has been a settlement here for 1000 years. In Norman times it became the possession of Walter de Brunham – one of the knights who accompanied William the Conqueror. The area has echoes of even earlier periods, as the straight section along the wall of Holkham estate marks the line of a Roman road which linked a coastal fort to the larger settlement at Colkirk 12 miles inland.

REFRESHMENTS:

The Nelson Inn, Burnham Thorpe, at the start and finish of the walk. This inn is definitely different! Step inside and you will see why. It also has a good line in Nelson trinkets.

Walk 10   WRETTON AND STOKE FERRY $3^1/_2$m (5km)

Maps: OS Sheets Landranger 143; Pathfinder 921 and 900.
Field paths and an attractive riverside path.
Start: At 691999, Wretton Church.

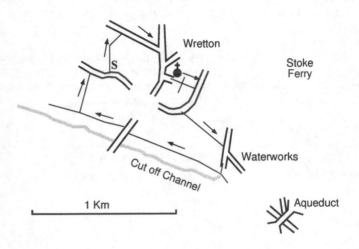

Go through the churchyard, walking to the right (south) of the church. Go through a gate and follow a path across the field beyond to reach a hedge. Go through a gap and continue with a hedge on your left to reach a road. Turn right and, just before the 40 mph sign and the next group of houses, turn left along a broad track (Limehouse Drove). On reaching a road opposite the waterworks entrance (to view aqueduct, continue ahead past the waterworks and turn right) turn right and, where the road ends, continue ahead between wooden posts to reach the bank of the **Cut-off Channel**.

Turn right along the bank. If you prefer you can walk along the top of the embankment, later descending to the bank. When you reach a bridge, go through the gate and turn right along the road. After 40 yards, turn left along a broad, signed track. After about $^1/_3$ mile (and 200 yards before a wood on the right), turn right along a track towards some rusty iron sheds, following it to reach a road. Turn right, bearing left and right with the road and, just after the last bungalow on the left, turn left along a signed track, walking with a fence on your left.

Go past another bungalow on the left and bear right with the track to walk along the left side of a ditch. Do not cross the earth bridge on the right: instead, continue with the ditch on your right to reach a road. Turn right and, at the next junction, turn right again. Now, just after a road junction on the left, opposite the telephone box, turn left along Church Path to return to the start.

POINTS OF INTEREST:

Cut-off Channel – The channel is part of the fens drainage system, connecting the River Lark at Mildenhall with the Great Ouse at Denver Sluice near Downham Market. At Stoke Ferry it crosses the Wissey on an aqueduct. Stoke Ferry, about $^1/_2$ mile from the start of the walk, was once an important town, being the only crossing point of the River Wissey and the undrained fens to the south for many miles.

REFRESHMENTS:

None en route, but there are possibilities at Stoke Ferry (which has an inn and a restaurant in a converted windmill) and at Wereham, about $1^1/_2$ miles to the north-west.

Walk 11   YARE VALLEY   4m (6¹/₂km)

Maps: OS Sheets Landranger 134; Pathfinder 903.
A peaceful river bank and parkland.
Start: At 203061, the Yare Valley Walk car park, Eaton Street,
Norwich.

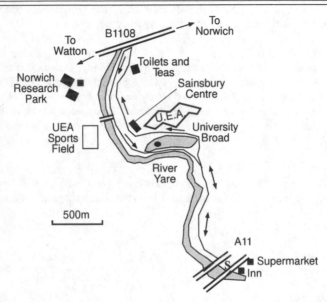

For this walk the Norwich City Tourist map, available from the Tourist Information
Centre, will be useful. The starting car park lies between Cringleford bridge and the
Red Lion Inn, on the opposite side of the road from the inn.

Leave the car park along the path adjacent to the information board/map. Follow the
path under the A11 dual carriageway and immediately turn left over a wooden
bridge. Turn right and follow a path, with the River Yare on your left, ignoring all
paths off to the right. After about a mile the path crosses a wooden boardwalk and
enters parkland at the southern end of **University Broad**. Here, turn right and walk
with the broad on your left, heading uphill on a track towards the **University of East
Anglia**, its building looking like a pile of egg boxes.

26

At a gate, turn left to walk along a second side of the broad, with the broad still on your left, now heading for the building on the skyline (the **Sainsbury Centre**) that looks like an aircraft hanger. Pass to the left of the Centre and head due north over Earlham Park to reach a road at the northern extremity of the park area, keeping football pitches to your left - especially if games are in progress. Ices, teas etc may be available from a café here, but it has seasonal, and restricted, opening.

At the end of the park, turn left, downhill, to reach the riverbank. Turn left and follow the river back through the park into the UEA grounds. The buildings to your right, across the river, are the Norwich Research Park - hi-tech science establishments which include sugar beet and food research. The animals grazing on the far bank belong to the UEA School of Rural Development which researches Appropriate Technology for the Third World. The mule you may spot pulls state-of-the-art ploughs, as do the oxen.

When you reach the broad, keep this to your left and, at its southern end, turn right along the boardwalk you entered on. Now reverse the outward route along the river bank back and under the A11 to return to the car park by the old Cringleford Bridge.

POINTS OF INTEREST:

University Broad – As with all the other Broads, this is man-made. It is home to many water birds and was also the capture spot of a Red-eared Terrapin - possibly a pet released when the 'Ninja Turtle' craze died. Such creatures can give a nasty nip which may be the reason for the 'No Swimming' notices here.

University of East Anglia – A postcard depicting the UEA as seen from University Broad won first prize in *The Ugliest Postcard* competition run by Glasgow University Students.

Sainsbury Centre – Surprisingly, the Centre is not a museum devoted to the retail food industry, but home to an excellent collection of tribal and modern art - courtesy of the Sainsbury family. It is open to the public: there is an admission fee.

REFRESHMENTS:

The Red Lion Inn, at the start.

Also available at the Sainsbury Centre and, sometimes, from the cafe in Earlham Park.

Walk 12   POTTER HEIGHAM AND HICKLING BROAD   4m (6km)

Maps: OS Sheets Landranger 134; Pathfinder 863 and 884.

A 'Swallows and Amazons' exploration of Broadland birds and butterflies.

Start: At 419199, Potter Heigham Church.

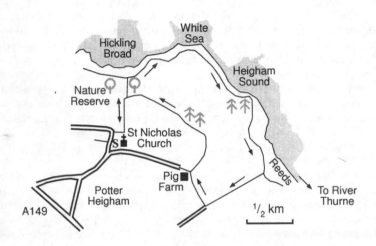

From **Potter Heigham** Church, follow Church Lane northwards and, where the road bends sharp left, turn right along a bridleway signed with Broads and County Council waymarkers: these are followed for the rest of the walk. Walk with a fence on your right and, after 50 yards, turn left to follow a wide, waymarked, green track towards woodland. At the edge of the wood, turn right, then, after 10 yards, go left over a stile into a **Nature Reserve**. Follow the path through trees towards **Hickling Broad**, cross a wooden bridge and, immediately beyond, turn right on to Weavers Way, following this clear path with open water and reeds on your left and carr woods on your right. The wooden hide sited over the path makes an ideal tea stop or rain shelter. You may care to bring binoculars for this stretch.

About 1¹/₂ miles after crossing the bridge, turn right where the path bends left and crosses a dyke via a gated wooden bridge (this is still on Weavers Way and there are waymarkers) to meet farm track. Turn right, following the track when it bends sharp right rather than the green lane (a bridleway) ahead. Follow your nose(!) towards and through a pig farm and, at its far side, fork right along a footpath. Follow this footpath, ignoring all turns to the right, into woodland. At the end of wood, cross a bridge and continue with a fence on your right. The path eventually returns to the entrance to the Nature Reserve: ignore the right turn into the Reserve and follow the track back to the road. Turn left to return to the start.

POINTS OF INTEREST:

Potter Heigham – (pronounced Potter Hi-am) was the site of a pottery in Roman times. The old bridge across the river here is medieval.

Hickling Nature Reserve – This is a National Nature Reserve managed by the Norfolk Naturalists Trust. Here can be found many marshland birds and the swallowtail butterfly. This area is an object lesson in the biological phenomenon of 'Succession'. Broads are manmade areas of shallow water, former peat diggings which have flooded. In the fullness of time, the water becomes shallower due to deposition of the products of nature (dead leaves etc). As these decompose they form a sort of soil. When the water is shallow enough, reeds can get their toes in and hasten the infilling process. Eventually enough soil is formed for scrub trees to survive - the willows and alders seen to your right. Man then takes a hand by cutting down the trees and draining the marsh to produce productive agricultural land - the grazing marshes seen just before the pig farm. Broadland today is a managed environment with the conflicting interests of farmers, conservationists and tourists all competing for a share of land use. You may spot a thatched cottage away to your left at the east end of the Reserve. This is a marshman's cottage. In past times these were the homes for those engaged in marsh management.

Hickling Broad – This is a desolate spot in winter, so, not surprisingly, there is a local ghost tale. A soldier skating across the Broad to visit his sweetheart one night hit a soft spot in the ice. The ice gave way and he slipped to an icy doom uttering the proverbial eerie scream. So, on a dark night, if you hear the swish of skates and see a tall figure in uniform…it's probably not the reserve warden!

The modern white sails seen to the east on this walk are a wind farm generating electricity.

REFRESHMENTS:
There is plenty of choice in Potter Heigham.

Walk 13   WESTON LONGVILLE   4m (6½km)

Maps: OS Sheets Landranger 133; Pathfinder 882.
A pleasant farmland walk.
Start: At 113158, Weston Longville Church.

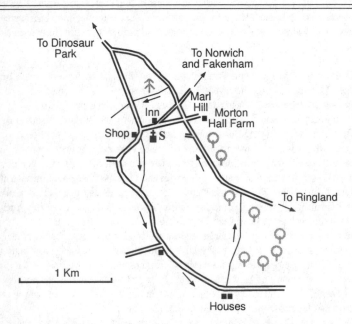

From the church in **Weston Longville** – opposite the Parson Woodforde Inn – turn left and take the enclosed/walled footpath on the left just after Church Farm Close. Follow the path to reach a minor road. Turn left along the road, ignoring a road off to the right, and, just before two houses on your right, where the road bends left, turn left along a gravel/sandy footpath (waymarked for the Circular Walk).

Follow the path to a minor road and turn left. Ignore a road off to the left, cross the main road and continue ahead along a road signposted for Lyng. After 250 yards, just beyond two derelict barns, turn left up a gravel track signed as a footpath. Follow the track between houses and then continue ahead along a clear path through a belt of trees.

At the far side of the trees, continue ahead, walking with a hedge on your left to reach a road. Turn left to a reach a junction and turn left there to return to the start.

POINTS OF INTEREST:

Weston Longville – The village was the home of the 18th-century diarist and *bon viveur* Parson Woodforde – hence the inn's recent name change. It was formerly the 'Five Ringers'. Woodforde's writings are a great insight into the eating habits of the clergy in his times.

Today the village is more famous as the home of Norfolk's one-and-only Dinosaur Park – just off the route. Transport of the beasts caused considerable consternation. Well – what would you think if a brontosaurus on a low loader went down your street?

This walk is popular with riders from the local livery yard, for the roads are quiet and the verges wide and full of wild flowers.

On the sandy soil of the area you will see many types of arable crops - including wheat, barley, linseed. You may even spot an artificial rainbow as the crop irrigators send a fine spray skywards. You may also see outdoor pigs - increasingly popular in East Anglia. These do very well on the light soil, but feel the heat and relish a muddy wallow on hot days.

The walk also has echoes of past agricultural practices. You cross Marl Hill: on light soils a Marl Pit was dug in the corner of fields. Soil from the depths was extracted and spread over the fields: the lowest levels were where nutrient minerals collected, having been washed through the soil by rain.

REFRESHMENTS:

The Parson Woodforde Inn, Weston Longville.

Walk 14   DITCHINGHAM AND BROOME   4m (6½km)

Maps: OS Sheets Landranger 134; Pathfinder 924.

Pleasant byways in the Waveney valley.

Start: At 342912, the Village Hall car park, Loddon Road, Ditchingham.

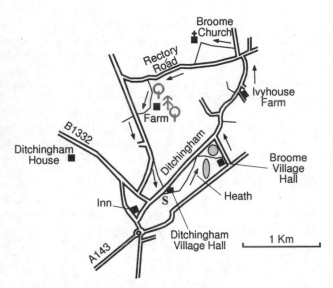

From the car park, take the footpath across the heath at the rear of the hall, passing between two sets of concrete posts. After 200 yards, at the corner of a wire-fenced area, turn left along another clear path, going under power lines to reach a road.

Turn right and, after 20 yards, at a signpost, turn right along a footpath, following it across a common to reach a road near the Broome Village Hall. Turn left to reach a T-junction. Turn right along the road, ignoring a road on the left and passing Ivyhouse Farm, on the right, to reach a crossroads. Turn left, then immediately right into Luggs Lane. After 5 yards, turn left along a footpath, following it across two fields to reach **Broome Church**.

From the church, follow a track to the road. Turn right and follow the road downhill, then, just before a ford, turn left over a stile and follow the wide track beyond along the edge of woodland. Continue along the track which, later, bears right and crosses a stream on stepping stones to reach a farm.

Pass the farm on your left and continue uphill along the track to reach a road. Turn left into **Ditchingham**. About 5 yards after the 30 mph sign, turn left along an enclosed footpath, following it to a road. Turn right to return to the start.

POINTS OF INTEREST:

St Michael's Church, Broome – The church stands at the original village centre. It boasts an organ that dates to Regency times and is still pumped by hand.

Ditchingham – The village was the home of the novelist Henry Rider Haggard, the Haggards living at Ditchingham House to the west of the village. Ditchingham Hall, two miles north of the village along the Norwich Road, was built in 1711 and has gardens designed by Capability Brown. It has restricted opening to the public.

REFRESHMENTS:

The Duke of York Inn, Norwich Road, Ditchington, just off the route.

Walk 15   **LYNFORD STAG**   4m (6½km)

Maps: OS Sheets Landranger 144; Pathfinder 922.

A pleasant Thetford Forest stroll. The paths are easy and passable by pushchair.

Start: At 813917, the Forest Enterprise car park, Lynford Stag, on the A134, 2 miles south-east of Mundford.

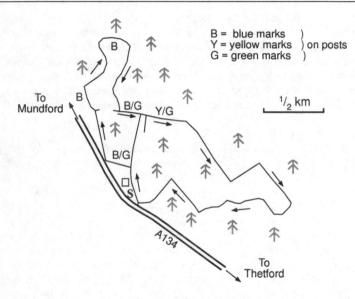

Note: This walk follows waymarked forestry routes through **Thetford Forest**. These are concessionary and may change with the needs of commercial forestry. The routes are waymarked with distinct coloured posts. At ride junctions look left, right and straight ahead for the next waymarker. The colours of the relevant posts are marked on the map for clarity.

Maps of all the forest's routes are available at the High Lodge Visitor's Centre and the Santon Downham Forest Office.

From the car park head northwards along the main track, following blue/yellow/green posts. At a cross-ride, turn left with blue/green posts. The ride later swings right to reach another cross-ride.

Turn left and, after 70 yards, turn right along a path with blue posts. This path cross a ride and then swings left. Turn left along the next ride, then follow a track back into the trees. Cross a ride, and then join another heading south.

Leave the ride at a blue post, bearing left into the trees to reach a crossing ride. Turn left and follow the blue/green/yellow posts to reach a crossing track. Keep straight on here, following yellow/green posts, ignoring the blue route leaving on your right.

Now ignore two rides off to the left to reach a cross-ride. Keep straight on following the yellow posts to reach the next ride. Turn left and, after 400 yards, turn right into the trees, following yellow posts. The path twists through the trees and crosses a ride: continue along it to reach another ride. Turn right to reach a cross-ride. Go straight across, then bear left through the trees to return to the start.

POINTS OF INTEREST:

Thetford Forest – This is the largest lowland pine forest in Britain. Planting first started in 1919, the year the Forestry Commission was founded to safeguard the nation's timber needs. In these more enlightened days, the amenity value of forests has been recognised and the Forest Enterprise arm of the Commission manages Thetford with conservation, education and relaxation in mind. With 1.5 million visitors annually, they seem to be getting it right!

Within the forest, large stands of Scots Pine are maintained to encourage red squirrels – the Park's emblem. Another emblem is the Lynford Stag, a stag-shaped sign at the entrance to the car park. This poor wretch was a target for shooting practice, belonging to the former owner of Lynford Hall. He still bears the scars.

REFRESHMENTS:

There is an ice-cream van at the start in season, but that is all on the route. There are opportunities in Mundford, 2 miles to the north-west, and in Thetford, 15 miles to the south-east.

Walks 16 & 17 ROYDON COMMON AND CASTLE RISING 4m (7km) or 10m (16km)

Maps: OS Sheets Landranger 132; Pathfinder 859.
Sandy heath, woodland, a nature reserve and an historic castle.
Start: At 697228, the Norfolk Wildlife Trust car park, Roydon Common.

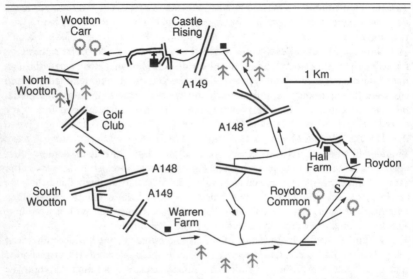

Cross the stile nearest the road and go through a gate on to an old railway track. Go left over a stile, cross a road and another stile, and go along a green track. At an industrial site go left across a field to a gate by houses. Go through, turn left and then right along the track opposite. Go between fences, uphill to a road. Walk ahead, passing Hall Farm and, just before a house, turn left along a road. Go past a white house and turn right along a broad track. About 200 yards after the hedge on the right ends, you reach a path junction.

The shorter route bears left here, then right along a broad track. Where the track turns right, go ahead to reach pine trees. Turn right over a stile, go left to the fence corner and left again to reach a road. Go left for 150 yards, then right along a signed sandy track. Turn left at a track junction, then right along a grey sandy track to reach a broad crossing track at the forest edge and turn left. The longer route is rejoined here.

The longer route follows the main track rightwards to reach the A148. Cross, with care, and go along the road opposite. Just after the field on the left ends, go right over a stile and take the left-hand track through woods to reach a hedge. Turn left to walk with the hedge on your right and cross a footbridge over a ditch. Go slightly left along an indistinct track to the left of three large trees and cross a footbridge to reach the A149. Cross, with care, to the signed path opposite and follow it between fields and past houses to reach a road at **Castle Rising**. Turn right and, just before the Black Horse Inn, turn right along a road. Go past the church and almshouses, then turn left along a signed path, walking with a fence on your right to reach a road. Walk ahead and, where the road turns left, bear right along a broad, signed track. Go through a gate and turn left at a barn. Now just before a house on right, fork left along a track, but where this bears left, go ahead along a path through trees to reach a road in North Wootton. Turn right, but soon cross the road and turn sharp left along a signed path. Immediately fork right and follow the main track, bearing away from the road. You will join a broad track: turn left and follow the main track with a sandpit on the left. At a sandy mound, bear right along a broad track, crossing a small stream to reach a track junction. Go left over a bridge and left again along a broad track. At the next cross-tracks, turn left, then immediately left again at a fork, continuing to a road near a golf club entrance. Turn right and, after 200 yards, turn left along a signed path. Join a broad track from the left and continue across fairways. At a white notice board beyond the last fairway go ahead, soon bearing right to reach the A148. Turn right, with care, then left into Sandy Lane. Where this road bears left, go ahead along a road, turning left with it to its end. Go ahead along a metalled path to the A149. Cross, with care, and go along the farm road, opposite, past the farm. Bear left, then go ahead, between fields, to reach the forest. Continue along a sandy track descending to meet a track from the left. The shorter route is rejoined here.

Continue eastwards, passing a white house and, just before a bridge, turn left over a stile on to a broad green track. Where the track narrows, bear slightly left along a narrow track between gorse. Cross a stile and walk ahead to regain the start.

POINTS OF INTEREST:

Castle Rising – The Norman castle has an ornamental keep surrounded by a circular earthwork. Queen Isabella was imprisoned here. Nearby is Howard Hospital, a group of almshouses founded in 1614.

REFRESHMENTS:

The Black Horse Inn, Castle Rising.

Maps: OS Sheets Landranger 132; Pathfinder 859.
An easy walk through woods and farmland.
Start: At 721225, the Bell Inn, Grimston.

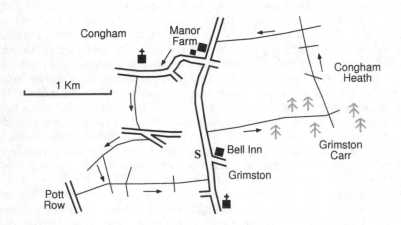

From the Bell Inn, turn right along the main street, heading northwards and passing the clock tower on your left. Just after the last house on the right, turn right along a broad sandy track signed as a bridleway. Where the track bears left after entering trees, continue ahead along a narrower track, passing tracks to both the left and right, to reach a cross-tracks by an enclosed pond. Turn left, then go ahead at the next cross-tracks to emerge from the wood. Go past a waterworks building on your left and, at the next cross-tracks, by a small wood on the right, turn left along a track towards farm buildings to reach a road.

　　　Turn left and, at a road junction, turn right along St Andrew's Lane. Continue through the village of Congham, passing the church on your right, and, at the telephone box, turn left along a field edge, walking with a hedge on your left. The track bears left, then right to continue with a hedge now on your right. At the field end, go over a stile and go diagonally across the field beyond aiming a few yards to the left of the far left corner. Go through a fence by way of a sliding fence panel and turn left along a broad track. After 25 yards, turn right over a wooden bridge and follow a track to an oak tree. At the tree, go right over a fence and walk along the left edge of a playing field, passing to left of a thatched pavilion. Go through a white gate and turn left along a road.

Follow the road around to the right and, at the 30 mph sign, turn right along a track, with gardens on the right. Where the hedges end, pass farm buildings on your right and, after passing a house on the right and a drive on the left, turn left along a signed path, following the field edge with a hedge on your left. At the field end, go slightly left through a gap and cross the next field just to left of telegraph poles. At a hedge corner (to visit **Pott Row** turn right and follow the path to a road) turn left across a field, heading to the left of a barn. Now walk ahead, with a ditch on your right, ignoring a footpath on the left. At the field end, cross a footbridge through a hedge and continue with a hedge on your right. Where the hedge ends, continue along the next field edge, heading towards a telegraph pole. On reaching the pole, bear slightly left, aiming for a small round-roofed barn just to the right of the hedge end, with a white house a little to the right. Pass to right of the barn and turn left along a road to return to the start in **Grimston**.

POINTS OF INTEREST:
Pott Row – The site lies about $^1/_3$ mile off route. The name derives from the local medieval pottery industry. A number of well preserved 13th-14th-century glazed green jars were found here in a well.
Grimston – Just to the east of the church is the site of a moated manor house.

REFRESHMENTS:
The Bell Inn, Grimston.

HOLT COUNTRY PARK 4$\frac{1}{2}$m (7km)
or 6$\frac{1}{2}$m (10$\frac{1}{2}$km)

Maps: OS Sheets Landranger 133; Pathfinder 841.
An interesting mix of forest, meadows and farmland.
Start: At 081377, the Holt Country Park car park.

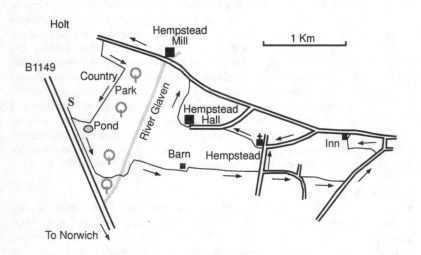

Go towards the car park entrance on the B1149 and, just inside, turn left along a wide track running parallel to the road, crossing a wide 'picnic table' stile at its end. Turn left, then, after 5 yards, turn right over a stile into a copse. Follow a narrow winding path to a stile and cross it into an open field. Cross the field on a well-marked path into conifer woodland. Head downhill along a wide ride, ignoring all paths off to left and right, and, at the bottom, cross a stile into a meadow. Cross an earth bridge over a stream (the infant River Glaven) and continue with a wire fence on your right. Turn left with the fence and, at the 'No Entry' sign, turn right up a wide track. Go over a rise and follow the track straight on to a barn. Turn left just beyond the barn, then, after 10 yards, turn right and walk with a hedge on your left. Turn right at the corner and, after 20 yards, turn left over a stile. Cross the large field beyond and enter Hempstead village along a green lane between houses.

The shorter route turns left here, along a road signposted for Holt on the Circular Walk. Turn left at a playground sign just before the church, going down a track towards 'The Old School Room' cottage where the longer route is rejoined.

The longer route crosses the road and goes ahead along Marlpit Road, signposted for Mannington on the Circular Walk. Where this road bends sharp right, turn left along a rough track, then, immediately, turn right again up wooden steps to reach a field. Cross the field to a road. Turn left and, just before the road bends right, turn left along a bridleway. Follow this into a field and walk with a hedge on your left to reach a stile. Cross this and the farm track beyond to reach a second stile into a meadow. Cross to the opposite hedge, turn right and walk to a stile. Cross to a road by an inn. Turn left, then first left into a road marked as Field Lane on the map, but Church Lane on the road sign. Follow the road to reach Hempstead village opposite the church. Cross the road and go down the drive leading to 'The Old School Room' rejoining the shorter route.

Bear right over grass then go through a kissing gate into a field. Turn right and follow a hedge as it swings left, then right, then left again. After another 10 yards, turn right over an earth bridge and continue in your original direction, with a ditch on your left. This section of the walk is waymarked. Follow the ditch to a wooden bridge and stile, crossing into a farm drive. Turn left and follow the drive to Hempstead Hall. Go into the farmyard and bear half-right through a gate into a field – the donkeys here are walker-friendly. Pass a pond on your right, then exit the field and head uphill, following the hedge on your right to a road. Turn left, passing **Hempstead Mill** on your left. At the top of the rise, opposite a deer warning road sign, turn left over a stile to return to the **Country Park**. Turn left and follow the main track to a pond. There, turn right and head uphill to the car park.

POINTS OF INTEREST:

Hempstead Mill – The flour ground here must have been of dubious quality for the bakery on site used to buy in flour supplies!

Holt Country Park – The Park has a vigorous Ranger. In summer you may join school parties discovering the delights of Stinking Willies (fungi).

REFRESHMENTS:

There is an inn, *The Hare and Hounds*, on the longer route and an ice cream van, in season, in the Country Park.

Walk 21   **BACONSTHORPE CASTLE** $4\frac{1}{2}$m (7km)

Maps: OS Sheets Landranger 133; Pathfinder 841.

Quiet country tracks around an historic monument.

Start: At 121380, the Baconsthorpe Castle monument car park.
Follow the road signs from the village.

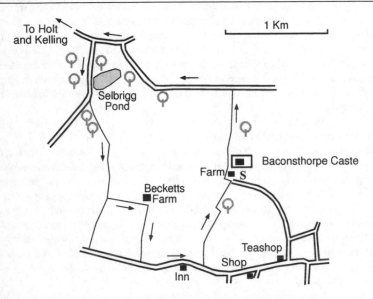

After a browse around the ruins of **Baconsthorpe Castle**, exit the car park and turn
right towards some farm buildings. Go between two barns and, at the end of the cow
barn on your right, turn right and go through a gateway into a field. Now, keeping a
hedge on your left, walk downhill (heading roughly northwards) and, at the bottom
of the hill, go through a gate and a small wood to reach a rough track. Walk ahead
along this track, going uphill to reach a minor road. Turn left along the road bearing
right with it to reach a junction. Turn left here, then take the first turning left, along a
minor road signposted Hempstead, walking with woods on your right. At the bottom
of hill, go past **Selbrigg Pond** on your left, continuing along the road until it bears
right. There, turn left up an enclosed, signed footpath along the left edge of the
woods.

Follow the path along the woodland edge, then cross a stile into a field. Cross the field on a well-marked path and turn right along the hedge on the far side. There is a waymarker here. Now walk with the hedge on your left through two further fields to reach, after 300 yards, a junction of tracks. Turn left up a rough track towards Becketts Farm. There, turn right on to a less rough track and follow it to a minor road.

Turn left along the road, passing the Hare and Hounds Inn on your right. About 300 yards after the inn, turn left along a signed footpath, crossing a field to reach a gap in the far hedge. The wire fence here is covered with grey alkathene pipe so look for the grey splodge in the far hedge. Go through the hedge and continue ahead, with a second hedge on your left. Ignore a gap in this hedge halfway along the field and, at the corner, turn left through a gateway. After about 20 yards, turn right on to wide farm track – there is a copse on your right – and follow it back to Baconsthorpe Castle.

POINTS OF INTEREST:

Baconsthorpe Castle – This is a 15th-century manor house built by the Heydon family. The family were sheep farmers but sheep owning in those days was far from the gentle 'One man and his Dog' image of today, for the manor house was fortified. The monument is managed by English Heritage and is open between 10am and 4pm.

The large white object dominating Baconsthorpe village is a water storage tower, a common sight in East Anglia where water supplies are largely derived from the underlying chalk aquifer.

Selbrigg Pond – This was a duck decoy where wild ducks were attracted to land by the sight of a trained decoy running up and down. Little did they know that this was all a cunning trap...

The stream at Selbrigg pond is the infant River Glaven which meets the sea between Blakeney and Cley.

REFRESHMENTS:

The Hare and Hounds Inn, Baconsthorpe.

There is also a large choice in the nearby town of Holt, 4 miles to the west.

Walk 22   **STOKESBY** $4\frac{1}{2}$m (7km)

Maps: OS Sheets Landranger 134; Pathfinder 884.

A 'Swallows and Amazons' landscape of sky and marshes.

Start: At 431106, the car park adjacent to the Ferry Inn, on the Staithe, Stokesby.

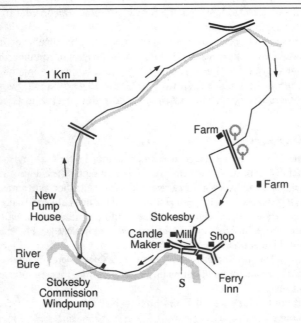

From the staithe, turn your back on the river and cross the Green to a road. Turn left and, after 50 yards, just before the Candle Maker and the Mill, turn left along an enclosed footpath with a green arrow, the Broads Authority waymarker. Follow the path as it bends right at the back of the candle shop and then follow the clear path along the riverbank.

In $\frac{3}{4}$ mile you will pass Stokesby Commission Windpump on your right. Just before the modern **water pump**, turn right away from the river along a clear path which follows **Muck Fleet**, on your left initially, but then on your right, to reach a road.

Cross the road and continue along a clear, waymarked path with the dyke still on your right. After $1^1/_2$ miles the path joins a farm track: continue straight on and, after a further 200 yards, at a waymarker, turn right, off the track, and continue with the dyke on your left.

Follow the waymarked track as, later, it goes into tall trees. Leave the trees and cross a farm drive, then cross a field to a waymarker post. Turn left along a green track under the power lines and, after 300 yards, where a hedge starts, turn right and walk with the hedge on your left.

At the end of this hedge, turn left and follow an old treeline, on your left, for 150 yards to reach a yellow topped post. There, turn right across a field, heading towards some houses.

Follow an enclosed footpath between the houses to reach a road. Go straight on to reach the **Stokesby** Village Green. Cross the road, and then the grass, to return to the start.

POINTS OF INTEREST:

Water Pumps – This area is very much a managed environment and is now an Environmentally Sensitive Area, with farmers being paid to maintain the fields as grazing marsh. Without pump systems these fields would flood. In times past this drainage was carried out by wind power – hence the many mills, one such being the Stokesby Commission Windpump. Today the same job is carried out by electricity. The modern site on the Bure drains 5200 acres. For those with an engineering turn-of-mind the shed houses two Archimedes screws which can each shift 9000 gallons a minute into the Bure.

Muck Fleet – It is not as bad as its name implies, as it is home to many insects including the rare Norfolk Aeshna dragonfly. It was once the dividing line between two Hundreds, the old administrative districts of the area.

Stokesby – The village is an ancient settlement; its Norse ancestry being shown by its name – the suffix 'by' is the give away.

REFRESHMENTS:
The Ferry Inn, Stokesby.

Walk 23   HUNSTANTON AND OLD HUNSTANTON   4¹/₂m (7km)

Maps: OS Sheets Landranger 132; Pathfinder 818.

A seaside and country Walk with historical interest.

Start: At 677406, the car park at the rear of the Hunstanton Council Offices.

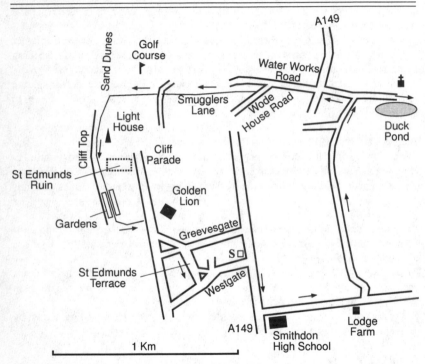

From the car park, walk along Westgate, soon joining the A149. Turn right, with care, walking southwards on the far side of the main road to reach Downs Road, on the left, just before the Smithdon High School. Take that road, following it past Lodge Farm and then taking the first track on the left. Follow the track to reach a road coming in from the left, then go ahead along that road, which soon bends to the right to join another road coming in from the left. At this point a seat is provided for a pause or for refreshments.

Turn right past the attractive duck pond to reach **St Mary's Church**, the family church of the Le Strange family. Return to the duck pond and walk straight ahead to reach the A149. Cross the main road, with care, and follow Waterworks Road to reach Wodehouse Road on your left. Follow Wodehouse Road, but soon bear left along a gravel path known as Smugglers' Lane. Follow the path across the access road for a golf club, then cross the golf course, beware of flying golf balls, to reach a beach.

Turn left towards the lighthouse then climb the path to the cliff car park and, following the cliff path, pass the lighthouse, on the seaward side, and the remains of St Edmund's Chapel. Keeping to the open groundon the cliff top. enter the cliff gardens. Cross the green at the Golden Lion Inn to join St Edmund's Terrace. Follow this around to Westgate and continue back to the Borough Council Car Park.

POINTS OF INTEREST:
St Mary's Church – This is the family church of the Le Strange family, the churchyard holding the graves of several members of the family as well as the graves of two men killed by smugglers. Just beyond St Mary's, going south, is Hunstanton Park, the estate of the Le Strange family. It is open to the public on Thursdays and makes a worthwhile extension to this walk.

REFRESHMENTS:
The Golden Lion, The Green, Hunstanton.
There are also other possibilities in Hunstanton and Old Hunstanton.

Maps: OS Sheets Landranger 144; Pathfinder 943.
Breckland, heath and woods on the Suffolk border.
Start: At 956806, Knettishall Heath Country Park.

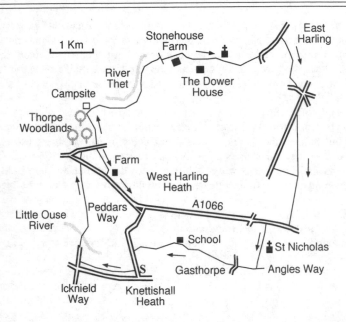

Leave the car park by the start of a woodland trail, heading westwards, following the 'Red Rabbit', then 'Green Rabbit', trails backwards. Go through the wood to a waymarker post and turn right along Peddars Way. Cross a bridge over the Little Ouse and turn left along a narrow path through trees. Continue with an open field on your left, then go through scrub, with the field now on your right. Cross the A1066, with care, and continue along Peddars Way. At the next road turn right, leaving the Way, to reach the Thorpe Woodlands campsite on the left.

The shorter route turns right here, following a signed grass track, towards a farm. Turn right at the farm to reach the A1066. Turn left, with care, then right at a junction to return to the starting car park.

The longer route turns left along the road to the campsite. Go past the barrier and bear right around the site. Continue up a track signed with red topped posts (the NCC circular walk). Go past a campsite sign and, as the track bears left, bear right along a path through trees. Go right at a junction of paths then left at a T-junction, continuing through woodland. Go left at the next junction, continuing to follow the red topped posts, heading eastwards. Leave the wood, maintaining direction along a wide grass track, with Scots pines on the left. The track meets a second wide track at the end of a clearing on the right. At the junction, turn left, maintaining direction through the next clearing. The track bears right through trees to reach a T-junction: continue ahead, bearing left, then right, with a field on the left, to reach a track. Cross to reach Stonehouse Farm. Continue ahead ignoring a signed path to the right. Go through a gate and walk ahead, with farm buildings on your right. Do not turn right into the farm: instead, go ahead through two gates and, as the track turns left, turn right through a signed gate. Cross a stile and turn left over a second stile. Go across the field beyond to reach a line of electricity poles by the wood opposite. Cross a plank bridge and stile and follow a path through trees. Cross a campsite towards a house and, at the end of the drive, go through a fence and follow a path through trees. Cross a wire fence and the field beyond to reach a track around a church. At the corner of the churchyard, turn right along a grass track towards buildings to reach a wide track. Turn left, go past a 'private' sign and turn right at a junction to reach a road at The Lodge, on the left. Maintain direction along the road into the village of Middle Harling. Just after the last houses on the right, turn right over a signed stile and go along the right edge of a field. Go over a stile and continue ahead to reach a road. Turn left, then right at a junction. Now, just past a turn to the right, turn left along a signed path, with a hedge on your right. Cross a stile and turn right, with care, along the A1066. Just before the flint house on the left, turn left along a signed broad track between trees. Continue along the left side of a field. On the left in the second field are the remains of the 14th-century St Nicholas' Church. On reaching a track by a gate, turn right through the gate (Angles Way) to reach the village of Gasthorpe. Bear left (waymarker on a pole by the phone box) and continue ahead between thatched cottages ('private road' and footpath signs). Go past a house on your left, then the church on your right and the school on your left, and go through the school grounds to reach a junction. Bear left to a road. Turn left to return to the car park.

REFRESHMENTS;
Nothing en route, but there is a (seasonal) Ice Cream van at the start and possibilities in nearby Thetford (5 miles to the west) and *The Fox Inn* at Garboldisham (3 miles to the east).

Walk 26   **BEACHAMWELL**   4½m (8km)

Maps: OS Sheets Landranger 143 & 144; Pathfinder 900.

Typical Breckland landscape with conifers, farmland and open views and an interesting village.

Start: At 751053, St Mary's Church, Beachamwell. Cars may be parked on the grassy area to the south of the church.

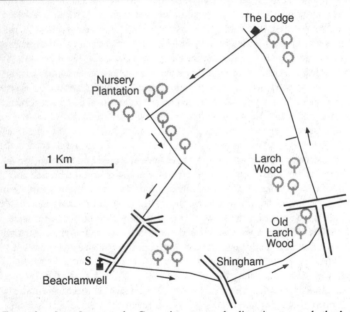

From the **church**, cross the Green in an easterly direction towards the **inn**. Cross the grassy area to the right of the inn, walking with a fence on the left and go over a stile. Turn left along a farm track for a few yards, then turn sharp right along a field edge, walking with a fence on the right towards a wood. Follow the path through thewood, with a field and then a grassy area with trees just to your right. Where the wood ends, cross a footbridge over a ditch and bear slightly right across the field beyond, aiming for the wooden finger post just visible at the far corner, just to right of a white house (one of two). At the field corner, cross a road and bear slightly left down a broad track, with houses on your left.

The track soon bears right, and then left: continue along it, passing a track on the right at the first bend and continuing to a wood, bearing slightly left between fences to reach a road. Turn left to reach a junction. Go straight ahead along a track signed as a bridleway, following it to a fork. Take the right branch, leaving a house on the left.

Go past a track on the right and continue ahead between fences to reach a gate. Go through and continue, passing another track on the left and walking with a fence on your right to reach trees. There, go right, then left with the track to reach a gate. Go through and continue ahead, with a plantation on your right. The track now bears left, then right through the trees. Take left branch at a fork by a telegraph pole and then turn left along a crossing track. Go past a house on the right and continue ahead along a broad, stony track to reach trees on the right and, later, a wood on the left. At the edge of the wood, turn left along a field edge, keeping the wood on your left. At the far end of the wood, turn right along a track towards farm buildings. At the farm, continue ahead along a metalled road to reach a junction. Go ahead to reach the village inn, turning right there to return to the church and the start.

POINTS OF INTEREST:

Church – Although it is only a small village, Beachamwell possessed three medieval churches. St Mary's, the remaining church, has a Saxon tower and a thatched roof, while the remains of St John's ($\frac{1}{2}$ mile north-west) and All Saints' ($\frac{1}{2}$ mile south) can still be seen.

Inn – In contrast to the churches, there is only one village inn, but this compensates by having two names (The Great Dane's Head and the Hole in the Wall) and two illustrated signs. Indolent drinkers can have a drink in both without moving.

REFRESHMENTS:

The Great Dane's Head and *The Hole in the Wall*, Beachamwell. Both serve meals (with identical menus!).

Walk 27   HINDOLVESTON   4¹/₂m (7km)

Maps: OS Sheets Landranger 133; Pathfinder 861.

A walk through a tranquil agricultural area – a place where verges are wider than the roads.

Start: At 040294, the car park at the Village Hall, The Street, Hindolveston.

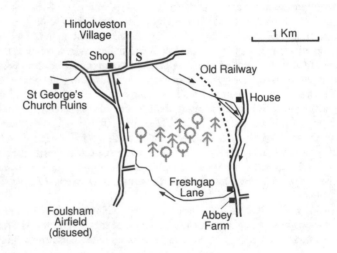

From the Village Hall, head eastwards along The Street and, after 200 yards, opposite Manton Grange, turn along a footpath/track on the right. After a further 100 yards, at a footpath signpost, turn left into a field and follow its left edge. Cross a stile in a hedge and follow a ditch on your right. Cross an earth bridge after 50 yards and continue with the ditch now on your left.

After 800 yards turn left along a signed footpath and cross a raised (old) railway track. Descend and turn right over a stile. Now ignore a footpath over stream (after 20 yards) keeping straight across the field (bearing 130°). Maintain direction through a gate and across the next field. Go through a gate and follow the hedge on your right to go over a stile and bridge and go up steps to reach a road.

Turn right and, after ³/₄ mile, at Abbey Farm, turn right along Freshgap Lane, a footpath. At the end of this track, keep ahead, walking with a hedge on your left. Cross a stile and walk straight across the field beyond. Cross a plank bridge in a hedge gap and maintain direction across the next, small, field. Cross a bridge and turn right along a concessionary path, following it to reach a green lane. Turn left and 200 yards before reaching a house and road, turn right along another concessionary path, heading towards a wood. At the wood turn left along a track to reach the road.

Turn right, ignoring a minor road to the left to reach a T-junction in **Hindolveston** village. Turn right to return to the start.

POINTS OF INTEREST:

Hindolveston – The village has some lovely old buildings. It is worth exploring the ruins of St George's Church. You may spot the stump of the village windmill and the bakery with loaves and fishes on the wall.

This part of Norfolk is one of the quietest in the county since it is far from the honeypots of the coast and the Broads. The only sounds you are likely to hear are the drone of insects and the distant hum of combine harvesters. It was a very different story in 1942 when Foulsham Airfield (to the south-west of the walk) was operating. Lancasters, Wellingtons, and Mosquitos flew from here. Horsa gliders were also stationed at Foulsham – a far cry from the modern leisure birds.

REFRESHMENTS:

None en route, but there is an inn and a shop in Foulsham 3 miles to the south, and numerous opportunities in Melton Constable 4 miles to the north.

Walk 28   OVERSTRAND   5m (8km)

Maps: OS Sheets Landranger 133; Pathfinder 842.

A bracing cliff top walk with a possible sightseeing extension into Cromer.

Start: At 247411, the Pay and Display car park, Cliff Road, Overstrand.

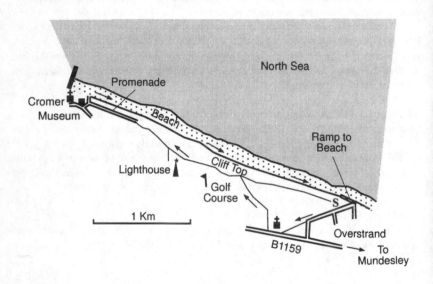

From the car park turn right along the road (Pauls Lane), following the Circular Walk waymarkers - dark green arrows with yellow feet. As the road bends sharp left, turn right along an enclosed footpath, leaving the Circular Walk. At the path's end, turn right along the main road (the B1159), with care, passing a church on your right.

After 200 yards, just after a Convalescent Home, turn right along a footpath, following it down the right edge of a field and on to a golf course. Bear half-left across the course, heading towards steps and continuing uphill towards a flagpole.

At the top of the hill turn left to follow a well-marked path running parallel to the cliff, hopefully avoiding both low flying golf balls and cliff edge! The cliff edge is the more hazardous: this area is poorly consolidated Boulder Clay left by the last Ice Age, and is crumbling rapidly.

The path passes Cromer lighthouse (on your left) and then enters **Cromer** town via the Promenade. After passing the pitch and putt course, the path swings left, then right. At its end, turn right along The Gangway, going down the steep boat ramp to the beach. The lifeboat museum here is worth a look.

Turn right along the beach for 2 miles to reach Overstrand. If it is stormy or the water is high it is best to retrace the route along the cliff top. At the concrete ramp at **Overstrand**, turn right, off the beach, going up a ramp to reach a road at the cliff top. Turn left here for Fishermen's Café or right to return to the car park. Going straight on allows the purchase of fresh boiled crab or lobster in season, March to October, from fishermen in The Londs.

POINTS OF INTEREST:
Overstrand – The village was made famous by the writings of Clement Scott at the turn of the century, though he called it 'Poppyland'. Locals refer to the village as the 'Village of Millionaires' due to the number of wealthy people it attracted to live in the area. A browse through the village will reveal some of their dwellings, including 'The Pleasaunce' which was designed by Lutyens with gardens by Gertrude Jeckyll. The grounds are occasionally open to the public.
Cromer – This is a down-to-earth fishing town, though is still worth exploring. The Museum adjacent to the church has an interesting display on local history and geology. Hunt out the West Runton Elephant - a fossil mammoth recently extracted from the cliff at West Runton.

REFRESHMENTS:
Both Overstrand and Cromer have numerous opportunities. There is an ice cream van in the starting car park during the summer, and Overstrand's Fishermen's Café is cheap and cheerful and its meals very filling.

Walk 29   CAISTOR ST EDMUND   5m (8km)

Maps: OS Sheets Landranger 134; Pathfinder 903.

Exploring the ancient capital of Norfolk.

Start: At 233034, the Norfolk Archaeology Trust car park, Caistor Roman Town.

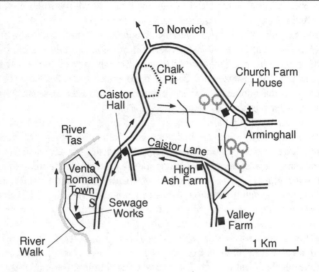

From the car park, head north-westwards towards Norwich's southern bypass following the green-arrowed Riverside Walk. This walk takes you west through water meadows, then heads southwards, passing a sewage works, before backtracking northwards along the River Tas. Eventually the walk enters the site of **Venta Icenorum Roman Town** on its north side. Explanatory boards give details to help you browse.

Leave the Roman Town along a gravel track to the left of the church. At a minor road, turn left towards Norwich. There is no pavement here but there is a wide verge on the left. Go straight on at the crossroads beyond Castor Hall and, after a further 550 yards, turn right through a green metal gate and go along a gravel track. (There is a footpath sign very high up on telegraph pole opposite and a **Norwich Fringe Project** waymarker on the gate post.)

Follow the track uphill for 1200 yards to Arminghall village, ignoring all paths off to both left and right. The track joins a gravel drive to some houses: continue ahead along this drive with houses on your right and, at a minor road, turn left to pass Arminghall Church on your right. At Church Farm House (on the left) turn left up the drive (there is a footpath sign) and, after 30 yards, at the 'Private Drive' sign, turn left into a field. Walk with a hedge on your left to reach the green sunken track used earlier in the walk. The path to this point is not as on the Pathfinder map, but is waymarked. Turn right along the green track, but, after 30 yards, turn left along a footpath signposted for Caistor Lane. Walk with a hedge on your left, going downhill through two fields. Go past a wood on your left and, about 20 yards after its end, turn left over a wooden bridge (there is a Norwich Fringe Waymarker). Continue with the stream and wood on your left, and, at the end of the hedge on your right, turn right, uphill, towards a house. Enter the garden along a clear path and follow the wire fence on your left to a road.

Turn left, then, after 100 yards, turn right at a footpath sign for Valley Lane. Go over a sleeper bridge and follow the hedge on your left as it swings left, right, right and left into a second field. Continue, with the hedge still on your left, to reach a road. (This sounds complicated, but is waymarked and well used.) Turn right along the road, going uphill to High Ash Farm and a T-junction. Turn left (Caistor Lane). Ignore the road to the left at the bottom of the hill and, at the main road, with Caistor Hall on your left, turn left back to the start.

POINTS OF INTEREST:

Venta Icenorum – The name means 'Market Place of the Iceni'. Construction was begun around 70AD. The site was a large Roman garrison town and a major port - the River Tas was larger at that date. The descendants of the Iceni have extracted their revenge on the Romans for little remains of the town now, the stones have long since been appropriated for, perhaps, more mundane buildings.

Norwich Fringe Project – This is a County Council initiative to develop the network of paths close to the City of Norwich. They have done a good job here! There are good views of the area from the ridge around Arminghall. Arminghall Henge is close by, a religious site dating to at least 2000BC.

REFRESHMENTS:

Nothing on route but there is an inn 1 mile up the road in Stoke Holy Cross and plenty of choice in the nearby, more modern Market Place of the Iceni - Norwich. Caistor Hall has a bar and restaurant, but it is rather smart for walking kit.

Walk 30 NORTH WALSHAM PARISH WALK 5m (8km)

Maps: OS Sheets Landranger 133; Pathfinder 862 and 842.

A pleasant farmland stroll.

At 282297, the Railway Station car park, North Walsham.

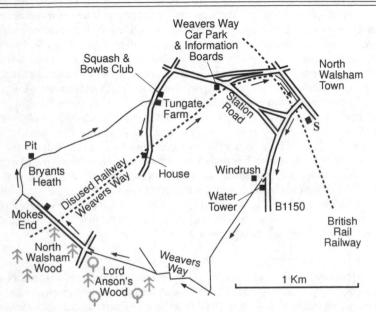

From the car park, cross the road and turn left along Norwich Road. Go past the Baked Bean factory on your left and continue to the large **water tower**. There, turn right along a track signed **North Walsham** Parish Walk. You will be following these waymarkers for most of the rest of the route.

Go past Windrush bungalow on your right and enter a field. Cross to the far right corner to reach a square pond and a waymarker post. Continue ahead, with a hedge on your left, to reach the junction of four tracks. Turn right (signposted for the **Weavers Way**) along an enclosed green lane. When the green lane ends, continue ahead, with a hedge on your right and a daffodil field on your left. Follow the hedge as it bends right, then left and, at the end of the field continue ahead along a well-marked bridleway with a wood on your left (you are still on Weavers Way). Ignore a footpath off to your right after 200 yards, continuing with the wood (**Lord Anson's**

Wood) on your left to reach a road. Cross and continue up the 'dead end' road ahead, still with woodland on your left.

Go under a disused railway (Weavers Way leaves our route here), pass Mokes End on your right (admiring the donkeys) and, at the end of the road, continue ahead along a track on to heath. At a T-junction turn right – there is a Parish Walk waymarker – and follow the waymarked path through the heath, passing a sand pit on your left. At the T-junction on the far side of the pit, turn right (waymarked) and leave the heath, continuing along a wide headland between two fields. Walk with a hedge on your left and, at the field corner go straight on, heading towards a red roof in the distance. At a hedge and waymarker post, continue in same direction heading for the left of the buildings to reach a minor road.

Turn right, then, after 400 yards, turn left back on to Weavers Way. Here the Way follows a disused railway track. Follow the trackbed back into North Walsham. Follow Weavers Way as it crosses Station Road and, at the end of the track, at a T-junction, turn left. Go through a metal barrier and turn right to pass under the railway bridge. Now, just before a road bridge crosses your path, turn right along a tarmac track, following it with a road on your left and a railway, and then a park, on your right. At the traffic lights turn right to return to start.

POINTS OF INTEREST:

Water tower – The tower area was the site of a battle in the Peasants Revolt of 1381. It is said that 40,000 rebels met their end here. The Revolt was a response to an increase in Poll Tax! The leader, a local dyer named John Litester, was beheaded.
North Walsham – This was a prosperous town in the Middle Ages, its wealth based on the wool trade. Sadly, much of the town was destroyed by a massive fire in 1600 – hence most of the buildings date from the Georgian period when the opening of the Dilham canal and the coming of the railway brought prosperity again. The canal, which is no longer in use, linked the town with the Broads and the sea.

Further details of the Parish Walk may be found on a leaflet obtainable from local shops or the County Council.
Weavers Way – This is a 56-mile long distance path linking Cromer, on the north coast, with Great Yarmouth, on the east coast. In this area it follows the trackbed of the old M & GN railway.
Lord Anson's Wood – The Wood is named after the admiral who sailed round the World in 1740-1744.

REFRESHMENTS:
None on the route, but there is plenty of choice in North Walsham.

Walk 31　　　　**SHOTESHAM**　　　　5m (8km)

Maps: OS Sheets Landranger 134; Pathfinder 924.

A lovely farming valley walk along superbly kept footpaths.

Start: At 247991, All Saints' Church, The Street, Shotesham.

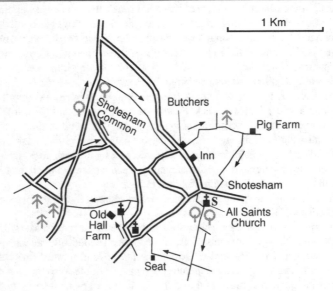

From the church, head downhill along Rogers Lane towards Saxlingham. Turn left along a footpath/track just before some white rails. Later this footpath becomes a clear path through woods: follow it through the woods, continuing along a path that goes uphill (southwards) across a field. Maintain direction with a hedge on your left and, at the end of the field, turn right and follow a mown path along the left edge to reach a seat. Turn right and continue downhill to a road. Turn left to reach a junction. Turn right and walk past the ivy-clad ruins of St Martin's Church. Turn right along a footpath just before **Old Hall Farm** to enter churchyard of St Mary's Church.

Leave the churchyard at the opposite right corner, following a path, with a hedge on your left. At the path's end, turn left, go over a stile and cross the field beyond along a clear path. Cross second and third fields in the same direction to meet a road at a junction.

Cross the road and continue ahead, downhill, along a minor road. Take the first road on the right (Knights Lane), following it to a T-junction. Turn left, then immediately right. At the next junction, turn left and, at the bottom of the hill, turn right.

After 300 yards turn right through a kissing gate on to **Shotesham Common**. Cross this south-eastwards: the actual route taken will vary with how wet the ground is. Leave the Common through a gate on to a road. Turn left to reach a T-junction. Turn right and, just after the butcher's shop, turn left along a bridleway. Follow the bridleway uphill, ignoring a track to the left at a wood, to reach a pig farm. There, turn right along a footpath.

Follow the path down to **Shotesham**, bearing left and then right with it as you near the village. Go round some houses to reach a road and turn right along it to return to the start.

POINTS OF INTEREST:

Old Hall Farm – The network of paths here are a shining example to all landowners. The owner, Mr Hazell, is a keen walker and manages the land to encourage wildlife whilst still running a business. Please respect his efforts.

Shotesham Common – The access gate was erected following a legacy to the parish - hence the notice on the kissing gate.

Shotesham – The village used to have four churches. Three remain - All Saints', St Mary's, with its wildflower churchyard: the unkept grass hides a wealth of orchids – please do not pick – and St Martin's, of which only the ruins remain. St Botolph's is preserved in memory only by house names.

REFRESHMENTS:
The Globe Inn, just off the route in Shotesham.

Walk 32   EARSHAM   5m (8km)

Maps: OS Sheets Landranger 134 and 156; Pathfinder 945 and 924.

A pleasant Waveney valley walk - history in every step.

Start: At 326888, Earsham Church.

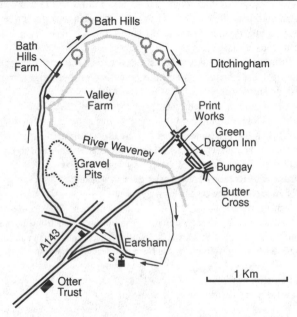

From the church, turn left along the road, then turn right up an enclosed footpath just after 19 Lodge Cottage. At the path's end, continue ahead along the pavement. Cross an estate road and continue along a path, going through barriers and passing the Village Hall on your left. Cross a road – the Queen's Head Inn is to your left – and continue up a 'dead end' road. At its end, take the footpath on the left side of the road, waymarked for Angles Way/Bigod Way, and follow it to the main A143.

Cross, with care, and continue ahead along a minor road signposted for Hedenham, Topcroft and Bedingham. Take the first turn right – a No Through Road – passing a gravel works, on your right, to reach Valley Farm. There, continue up a track (the Bigod Way), passing **Bath Hills** Farm.

Continue along a well-marked track for just over 1 mile, eventually descending through trees to a footbridge. Cross, then leave the trees and cross another narrow footbridge over the **River Waveney**. You are now in Suffolk.

Ignore a path to the right at a green arrow post (waymarked MAFF Environment Sensitive Area), continuing ahead along a clear path across a field to reach a gate and stile. Cross the stile and continue ahead along a track, crossing a footbridge and the meadow beyond to reach a kissing gate. Go through and turn left along a gravel drive to reach a roundabout on the A143. Cross, with care, and follow the main road into **Bungay**, passing a print works on your right.

Just after the Green Dragon Inn, turn right into Popson Road. Cross the road at the end and continue ahead to reach a T-junction. Turn left, then right into Earsham Street (or turn left for the Market Place, town services and Bigods Castle).

Leave Bungay, crossing back into Norfolk. Now, just before you reach grey rails on either side of the road, turn left along a footpath, walking with a dyke on your right. Follow the path as it turns right after $^3/_4$ mile, continuing with it to pass Earsham Mill and return to the church in **Earsham**.

POINTS OF INTEREST.

Bath Hills – The Romans grew grapes here. In Georgian times there was a spa bath, but, unusually, one with cold water! The author Ryder Haggard lived for a time in nearby Dersingham.

River Waveney – The river is the county boundary – hence North Folk and South Folk. The river here is in its senile, floodplain stage and, being sluggish and indolent, it drops its load of sand. Past deposits are extracted for building etc.

Bungay – This typical small market town, complete with a Butter Cross, is worth an exploration. The castle was built by Roger Bigod in 1294 – hence the name for the Town Trail which is a collection of walks in the vicinity.

Earsham – This is home to the Otter Trust, founded by the naturalist Phillip Wayre. Otters have been bred here and successfully released into the wild, including to sites in the Waveney valley.

REFRESHMENTS:

The Queen's Head, Earsham.

The Green Dragon, Bungay.

There is plenty of choice in Bungay and a tearoom at the Otter Trust, just off the route, near the start.

Walk 33   WICKHAMPTON AND HALVERGATE   5m (8km)

Maps: OS Sheets Landranger 134; Pathfinder 904.
A wilderness of sky, reeds and mills.
Start: At 427054, St Andrew's Church, Wickhampton.

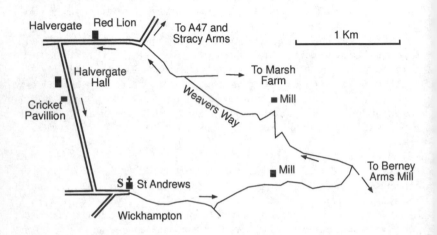

From the church, go down the gravel track towards the marshes. The track becomes concrete: stay with it, going through a gate. After a further $^1/_2$ mile, at a signpost for **Berney Arms Mill**, turn left, still walking on concrete. Go through a gate, beyond which the track becomes grassy. Follow this grassy track for just over a mile to reach a Weavers Way signpost.

There, turn left into a field and follow a clear track diagonally across it to reach a new wooden bridge. Cross and head for the iron gate in the far right corner of the field beyond. Cross the stile by the gate and turn right. You are still on the Weavers Way: follow the Way as it crosses a sleeper bridge and several stiles, then turns right towards a mill. At a field corner, turn left to cross further stiles and a concrete bridge. Now turn left along a track which is raised above the **marshes**, following it to a cattle pound.

Go through the pound and turn left along a track. Continue along this track when it becomes tarmac to reach a road junction. Keep ahead towards Halvergate village, still following Weavers Way. Go uphill, passing the Red Lion Inn on your right. Now, after a further 200 yards, turn left into Bakers Road. Keep ahead as this becomes Wickhampton Road. Go past the (derelict) Halvergate Hall, and the cricket pitch, enjoying the panoramic views over the marshes towards Great Yarmouth.

When you reach a T-junction turn left and, just after the telephone box, turn left to return to the church.

POINTS OF INTEREST:

Berney Arms Mill – This mill – built as a drainage mill in 1870 – is the tallest in Norfolk. During the summer it is open to the public.

Halvergate Marshes – These marshes were the subject of a fierce battle between farmers and conservationists in the 1980s. The marshes have been used for summer grazing for cattle and sheep for centuries. In the 19th century, cattle came from as far as Scotland to graze here. The grazing practises and peat-based soils have produced an unusual and rare environment which is home to many birds, orchids and grasses. Farmers, tempted by the high cereal prices in the 1980s, wanted to put this area under the plough. A massive public debate ensued which was finally settled by paying the farmers to maintain the grazing marsh as you see it today. The grazing agreements are managed by the Broads Authority, which is the local equivalent of a National Park Authority. Today many similar areas – Environmentally Sensitive Areas – have been set up countrywide.

REFRESHMENTS:
The Red Lion, Halvergate.

Walk 34   COCKTHORPE AND STIFFKEY   5m (8km)

Maps: OS Sheets Landranger 132; Pathfinder 819.

A walk for solitude: water meadows and the coast.

Start: At 981422, All Saints' Church, Cockthorpe.

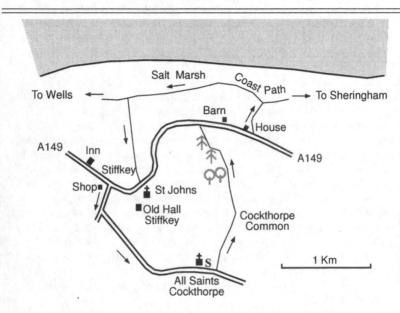

From the **church**, head eastwards along the road and, after 200 yards, just after the telephone box and just before a barn, turn left along a path signposted for Cockthorpe Common. At the end of this green lane, go through/over a gate/stile and continue on a clear path along the valley bottom.

Cross a wooden bridge and continue down an avenue of willows. Now cross a second wooden bridge and turn left along a clear path, walking with a dyke on your left. Follow the path through a belt of trees and continue to reach a road (the A149). Turn right, uphill, with great care, passing a barn, and then a house on the left, and continuing downhill.

Now, just before reaching some white rails/bridge, turn left along a footpath signposted for the Coastal Path. Walk with a dyke, then a fence and finally a hedge, on your right as you cross three stiles and head northwards to meet the Coastal Path.

Turn left along the Path, following it for a mile to reach an 'informal' car park. There, turn left, away from the sea, to go along a gravel track. Go past houses on your left and continue to reach the A149 opposite the church at **Stiffkey** village.

Turn right, downhill, again with great care, then take the first turn left, signposted for Cockthorpe. Cross a bridge and follow the road out of the village to reach a fork. Take the left branch towards Cockthorpe, following the road uphill. Ignore a turn to right, continuing along the road into Cockthorpe village to return to the start.

POINTS OF INTEREST:

All Saints' Church – This was the church where Sir Cloudesley Shovel and Sir John Narborough were christened. Both were famous admirals in the 17th century. Sir Cloudesley helped capture Gibraltar in 1704, while Sir John saw off the pirates terrorising the western Mediterranean.

Stiffkey – The village, known as 'Stewkey' to locals, had two churches until the 16th century as it was divided into two manors. The 'grave' of St Mary's remains as a mound in the churchyard of the surviving St John's. The Hall in Stiffkey was built by Sir Nicholas Bacon, a courtier of Elizabeth I.

Stiffkey used to be famous for its cockle sales – the cockles growing in the sands exposed at low waters just off the coast. These were known as 'Stewkey Blues', their splendid size and flavour being due, so it is said, to the effluent from the army camp in the village. Sadly, both the camp and the cockles are now gone.

REFRESHMENTS:

There is an inn, *The Red Lion*, just off the route in Stiffkey and plenty of choice in nearby Wells-next-the-Sea.

Walk 35   **WYMONDHAM**   5m (8km)

Maps: OS Sheets Landranger 144; Pathfinder 902.

Byways around an historic market town.

Start: At 111014, the Market Cross, now the Tourist Information Centre, in Wymondham Market Place.

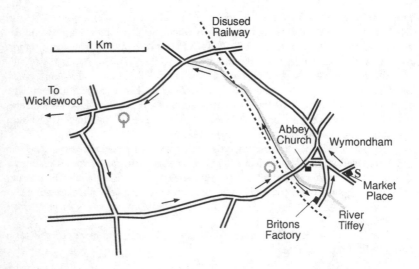

Follow Market Street downhill away from the Market Place, heading north-westwards and then turning left into Church Street at the town sign. Go past the Green Dragon Inn, then enter grounds of **Wymondham Abbey**. Leave from the far side of the churchyard on to a road. Turn left, go over a bridge and then, after 10 yards, turn right along a footpath into a field/Countryside Access Area picnic site.

Follow the enclosed path, with the River Tiffey on your right, for 1100 yards, then bear left over a disused railway and the river. Continue along a clear path, crossing two further footbridges and continuing into a picnic site by a road. Turn left along the road, following the road towards Wicklewood to reach a crossroads.

Turn left, then take the next left turn (Whitehouse Lane), following it for $^3/_4$ mile to reach a crossroads. Turn left towards Wymondham. Ignore a road to the right, continuing along the road to cross the railway. Now, after a further 10 yards, turn right into a picnic area.

Follow the clear path, with the River Tiffey on your left, to reach a road. Turn left to reach a T-junction, turning right there to return to the start in **Wymondham**.

POINTS OF INTEREST:

Wymondham Abbey – The Abbey was founded by the Benedictines, but after the Dissolution was demolished, only the church remaining. Rumour has it that a tunnel linked the monastery to The Green Dragon Inn - allowing the monks a chance to pop out for a crafty pint.

Wymondham – The town – the name is pronounced Windum – has more listed buildings than any other small town in Norfolk. Much of the early town was destroyed by a fire in 1615: the Green Dragon Inn is one of the earlier survivors. Perhaps the monks kept a guardian interest from heaven! The octagonal Market Cross building is only one of three in the country.

The town was once famous for weaving and for brush manufacturing. The site of Britons Brush Works is marked by a wall plaque opposite the White Horse Inn.

The walk is dominated by the twin towers of the parish church. One tower housed the bells of the monastery, the other the bells of the townspeople, the division following a falling out between the two parties. Sundays must have been rather noisy!

REFRESHMENTS:

The Green Dragon Inn, Wymondham.
There are numerous other possibilities in Wymondham.

69

Walk 36   NARBOROUGH AND MARHAM FEN   5m (8km)

Maps: OS Sheets Landranger 132 or 143; Pathfinder 880.

River bank, uncultivated fen and farmland.

Start: At 747130, Narborough Church.

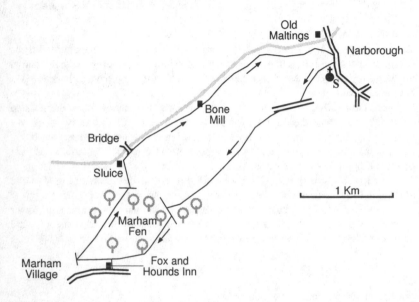

The church lies just off the A47. The nearest parking is in the layby in Marham Road: go about $^1/_4$ mile towards Swaffham and turn right at the bus shelter opposite.

From the church, go along the signed path by the stone wall to the right of the churchyard. Go through a gate and continue with a fence on your left. Go through a metal gate by the last bungalow and bear slightly left, following a track across a field, aiming to the right of some oak trees. At the end of the field, bear left over an earth bridge and go ahead along a track to reach a road. Turn right along a stony track (there is a bridleway sign), but where the track bears right, go through a signed opening on left, just past the first metal gate, and cross the field beyond, aiming for a very small gap in the treeline ahead, walking with an earth bank away to your left.

At the field edge, go slightly left through a gap in the trees and walk along the edge of the next field, following the fence on the left. At the next field end you join a track from left, continuing ahead with a ditch on your left. At the end of the second field, cross an earth bridge and bear slightly right across the field beyond, aiming to the right of a group of taller trees. Cross a metalled road, go through the gap opposite and follow the field edge, with a wood on your left to reach a metalled road. Turn left and, after 100 yards, at a crossing track, turn right through a metal gate and go along an earth track. **Marham Fen** is now on your right.

Follow the track for about a mile, passing an electricity sub-station on the left. The walk continues along the track to reach a track junction with a gate and a treatment plant ahead. Turn sharp right along a broad track with wooded fen now on both sides. After $^3/_4$ mile you emerge from the trees and go over a crossing track, bearing slightly left. Go past a brick building (sluice) on the left and turn right along the riverbank, going straight over at a cross-tracks, with a bridge on your left.

After $^1/_2$ mile you pass a disused water wheel on the opposite bank. This is the remains of **Narborough bone mill**. After a further mile, and shortly after the river forks (note the old maltings on the left), the path bears right at a fence, and then left to reach a road. Turn right and then turn left to reach the main road. Turn right, to return to **Narborough** and the start.

POINTS OF INTEREST:

Marham Fen – This is one of the few remaining areas of uncultivated fenland in Norfolk and houses many rare species of plants and insects.

Narborough Bone Mill – This was a thriving mill in the 19th century when bones were brought up the river from King's Lynn for grinding into meal. Only the wheel now remains.

Narborough – The village includes the remains of an old maltings and a well-preserved mill building adjacent to a trout farm.

REFRESHMENTS:

The Ship Inn, Narborough.

Walk 37   **FRING**   5m (8km)

Maps: OS Sheets Landranger 132; Pathfinder 839.

An attractive estate village, and easy tracks across the chalk farmland of High Norfolk.

Start: At 734342, on Peddars Way, $^1/_3$ mile south of Fring village.

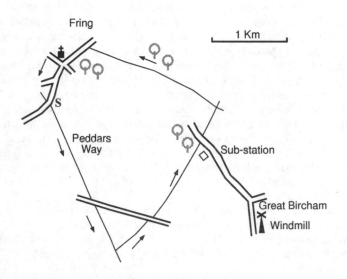

As there is no suitable parking in **Fring** village, the recommended starting point is the Peddars Way a few yards south of the point where it crosses the Fring-Shernborne road. Please park considerately.

Face towards Shernborne and turn left (southwards) along Peddars Way, which at this point, is a very broad track. Follow the track for nearly a mile – the Great Bircham windmill can be seen ahead to the left – to reach a road junction. Cross and continue ahead along Peddars Way for nearly $^1/_2$ mile. Now, just after passing a track to the right, and shortly before a wood, turn sharp left along the next track, walking downhill between hawthorn hedges to reach a road.

Cross the road and follow the track opposite, descending to a wooded hollow beyond a small brick building (a sub-station), on the left, to reach another road.

From this point a detour of about $^3/_4$ mile leads to the **Great Bircham windmill** – turn right along the road, then take the first narrow road on right. Return along the same route.

The walk continues by crossing the road (or turning right if you have made the detour to the windmill) and following an unmarked path along a field edge, walking with a hedge on your right. On reaching the field edge at the top of the hill, go through the hedge and turn left along a path, now walking with a hedge on your left. Shortly after the track bears slightly right to reach the next hedge: bear slightly left, go through the hedge, and turn left along the field edge, then follow the field edge around to the right, heading towards the left edge of the trees ahead. Continue ahead along a broad track to the left of a grey barn.

Follow the track downhill to reach a road. Turn left along the road, following it through the village of **Fring**. Go past one road, off to the right, and two, off to the left, continuing uphill to reach a road fork. Take the left branch to return to the start.

POINTS OF INTEREST:

Fring   This is a small estate village set below its 14th-century church. Church Farm, to the north of the principal street, is an attractive group of old buildings around a green.

Great Bircham Windmill – This is a beautifully restored, working windmill which is open to the public.

REFRESHMENTS.

None on the route but there are inns serving food at Sedgeford, Docking and Great Bircham, all of which are within 3 miles of Fring.

Walk 38   **BAWSEY AND LEZIATE**   5m (8km)

Maps: OS Sheets Landranger 132; Pathfinder 880.

A scenic walk through woodland and landscaped artificial lakes.

Start: At 673198, the main car park at Bawsey Pits.

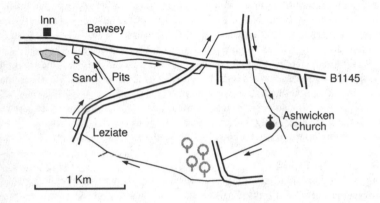

From the car park to the east of the lake, at **Bawsey Pits,** take the track by the 'take litter home' sign, into the wood. At the wooden exercise bar on the left, bear right along a track, with four wooden posts on the right. Go to the left of more exercise bars to join a track from the right, with a sandpit on the right. You will meet a track from the left: fork left away from pits and, at a cross-tracks, turn right towards a pit. Go left around the edge of the pit, and, at a clearing, bear left along a track through trees, heading away from the pit. At the top of rise you will meet a fence: turn left between fences, soon with a lake on your right. Go through a gap and, just before a road (the B1145), turn right along a path, walking parallel with the road, with a fence on your right. The path bears away from the road to meet another road: turn left for a few yards, then cross the road and turn left along a footpath. On reaching a gate on the right, turn left to join the road and turn right along it to its junction with the B1145.

Pass to the right of a triangle, cross the road, with care, and go straight ahead along the broad track opposite, walking between fields. At the field end by the power lines, turn right along the field edge and follow a track through trees. At the top of a rise, bear slightly left across a clearing to join a wide track. Turn right to reach a road and turn right along it to its T-junction with the B1145. Cross, with care, and continue ahead along the narrow path to the right of a metal rail. Where the fence on the right ends, bear right for 5 yards, then go left along the field edge, with a ditch on your left. At the field corner, bear slightly left over a footbridge. Cross the next field diagonally left to reach a hedge and turn right, uphill, towards a church. Where the hedge and ditch end, bear left to a narrow metal gate and footpath sign some way to the left of the church. Go through the gate, cross a track and go through the gate opposite. After a few yards, turn right along a broad track past a churchyard and then follow the track to the left. At an old quarry, go slightly left towards a tree gap at the far left corner. Continue over a rise and across a small field to reach a gate. Cross the stile to the left of the gate and go down the left side of the field beyond. Go through a gap in a hedge and maintain direction, walking with the hedge on your right. At the field end, go between houses to reach a road. Turn left and, where the road turns left, turn right along a broad track. After about a mile, bear right at a fork and follow a road to its end at a T junction in Leziate.

Cross the road and go through the gap opposite. At the top of a bank, turn right and, where the bank turns left, go ahead, through a gap by a gate. Cross a track and go through the gap opposite. Follow a path through trees, walking parallel with a road to reach a fence by a house. Turn left along a broad track and, where the fence on the left ends, bear slightly left, downhill, along a broad track with a lake on your right. Where the track bears right, turn left through a hedge gap, then go right along a track between fences. Go over bridge and continue to a fork. Take the right-hand, broad track downhill through trees to reach the start.

POINTS OF INTEREST:

Bawsey Pits – The old sandpits which have been turned into landscaped lakes (the area to the south is still worked) with adventure playgrounds and fitness trails.

Bawsey village is one of the smallest in Norfolk. The church, a picturesque ruin, stands more than a mile from the village in the middle of a field. It is visible from the King's Lynn southern bypass.

REFRESHMENTS:

None en route, but there is an inn at Bawsey, about $1/4$ mile from start. There is occasionally an ice cream van near the start on summer weekends.

Walk 39   **BRANCASTER**   5m (8km)

Maps: OS Sheets Landranger 132; Pathfinder 818.
A scenic coastal path, heath and a quiet country road.
Start: At 792445, Brancaster Staithe quay.

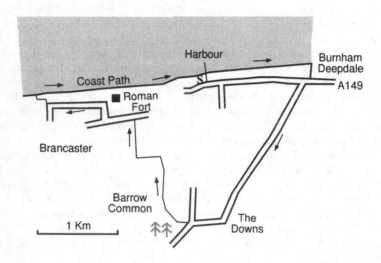

From the parking area by the National Trust barn in **Brancaster Staithe**, follow the coastal path eastwards for about 1 mile and, at a cross-tracks by a National Trust sign, turn right to join the main road (A149) at **Burnham Deepdale**. Turn right, with care, and immediately left along the road opposite. Follow the road uphill for $1\frac{1}{4}$ miles, then bear right with the road to reach a road junction. Turn right and then left along a narrow track that follows a wood edge.

The path bears slightly right, away from the wood, then right again, with a field on the left. At a track junction, bear slightly left with the path, go through a metal gate and continue downhill along the track beyond. Join a broad track by a gate and turn left to follow the track around to right. Continue downhill to reach the A149.

Turn left along the metalled footpath beside the road and, after about 300 yards (just after the 40 mph sign), turn right, with care, into Stockings Lane. Follow the road around to the left (noting the entrance to the **Branodunum** Roman fort at the bend). Where the road turns left, turn right along a gravel track and, after 30 yards, turn left on to a narrow path between fences. Go through a barrier and turn right along a road. When the road bears left, continue ahead along a track. Go through a gate and, at a crossing path, turn right along the Coastal Path and follow it back to the start.

POINTS OF INTEREST:
Brancaster Staithe – This picturesque harbour with moored boats and attractive cottages was once a busy port trading in grain and coal. The magnificent timbered barn is used as a National Trust visitor centre.
Burnham Deepdale – The village church has a Saxon round tower and a font decorated with the seasons of the year. Horatio Nelson, the hero of Trafalgar, was born at Burnham Thorpe, about 4 miles to the south-east.
Branodunum – This is the site of a Roman fort and settlement a short way from the sea.

REFRESHMENTS:
There are possibilities in both Brancaster Staithe and Burnham Deepdale.

Maps: OS Sheets Landranger 132; Pathfinder 839.
Woodland, coastal scenery and a disused railway line.
Start: At 685342, the village sign, Snettisham.

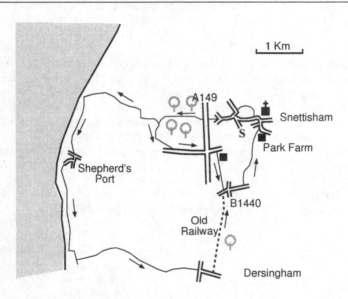

From the sign, turn right along the main street and immediately left into Alma Road. Opposite the surgery, turn right along a drive and immediately left through a gate. Follow the path beyond across a field to a gate to the right of a copse. Go over a footbridge and cross the main road (the A149) with care. Continue along the path opposite, between fences, for $\frac{1}{2}$ mile ignoring all side tracks. At the top of the hill, turn left with a track and go downhill and through a gate to reach a path junction.

The shorter route turns left here. Go through a gate after $\frac{1}{3}$ mile and continue ahead (ignoring a track on the left) to a road. Turn left, cross the main road (again with care) and follow the road opposite to a sign for Mill House and watermill. Turn right along the drive, passing the mill and sheds and continuing between fields. Cross a track and walk ahead along a field path. Do not join the old railway track:

instead, follow the field edge to join a narrow path between bushes. Cross two stiles to a road and turn left, rejoining the longer route.

The longer route turns right and, shortly, left along a track to the left of a barn. Bear right with the track to join a broad track. Turn left, bearing right, then left with the track, but where it goes left again, go ahead, over a stile. Bear slightly right across a field to the left edge of a hedge and follow a track to the left. Go over an earth bridge and maintain direction towards a metal gate. Go through and walk between small lakes to the top of an embankment. Follow the winding path opposite, then climb the next embankment and turn left along the shore path, following it for about 1 mile to Snettisham beach. Just before a car park, bear left down the embankment and follow a path to the left of a stream. Go to the left of the picnic tables, between posts and through a gate to reach a road opposite a caravan park. Cross and take the site entrance road, bearing right along a concrete track at a notice board (ignoring the private signs). At the road end, climb to the beach and turn left along the shore. About $^1/_2$ mile beyond the last bungalow, turn left (by a seat) and cross a lake by way of a causeway. Bear right with the track and, just before a stile, turn left over an embankment. Walk ahead, crossing a stream and concrete bridge and following a track, which soon becomes concrete, for about $1^1/_2$ miles to reach the main road. Cross, with care, and take the road opposite. Just before the first house, turn left over a stile on to an old railway track. Cross a grass track and continue along the track to a road. Turn right, rejoining the short route.

Follow the road to the B1440, cross, with care, and go along Hill Road opposite. Just after the last house on the left, turn left along a signed path, bearing left with the field on the right. At the end of the next field, go through a gap, cross a footbridge, and turn left along the field edge. Go over a bridge and through a kissing gate. Bear right across the next field to reach a signed bridleway at the corner of a small wood. Go through a gate on to an earth track, turn left. Go around to the right, but where the track bears right again, go ahead through a metal gate and follow a path between fences. Go through two more gates to join a broad track. Turn left at a road. Go ahead at a cross-roads, then follow a road to the left at the church. At the drive on the right for Hall Farm, turn right along a track (ignoring a footpath sign on the right) and follow the road to the left through a gateway. Go through a gate at the field corner and, where the track bears right by the last house, bear left along a path. Cross a field and go downhill to meet a track. Turn left, and left again at the road to regain the start.

REFRESHMENTS:
There are several possibilities in Snettisham.

Maps: OS Sheets Landranger 132; Pathfinder 840.
Heath, woodland and field paths.
Start: At 830326, the Lynn Arms, Syderstone.

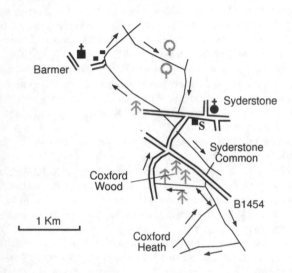

From the inn, turn left along the main village street and take the first road on the left. Shortly after passing a layby on the left (this is a convenient parking place) turn left along a clear path across the heath (Syderstone Common). Continue ahead at the first cross-tracks, but at the second, after about $^1/_2$ mile, turn right and follow the track to reach a road (the B1454). Turn left, with care, for 140 yards, then turn right along a gravel track (look for the footpath sign). When the track forks after a few yards, take the left branch through a gateway, passing a track on the right after a further $^1/_4$ mile. Now, where the wood on the right ends, turn right along a broad track, walking with a hedge on your right. On reaching another wood on the right, follow the track around to the right to meet another track after about 200 yards. Turn right. Where another track goes to the left, continue ahead through a gate and walk downhill between trees. At the crossing track turn left, retracing part of the outward route to reach another track junction, by the wood edge. Turn left and follow a track, with trees on your right, to reach a road. Turn right along the road to reach the main road (the B1454 again). Turn right, with care, then immediately left towards **Syderstone** village.

The shorter route now returns to the village, turning right to regain the start.

For the longer route, before reaching the village (or the layby passed on the outward route) turn left along a path directly opposite the one taken at the beginning of the walk. Follow this path around to right and, just before reaching a pond, bear left along another path, following it to reach a road. Cross the road and continue along the track opposite. Where the track ends by a house, continue straight ahead along a path between hedges, then go along the right edge of a field. Continue between hedges to reach a road at the hamlet of **Barmer**. Turn right and, after $^1/_2$ mile, turn right again at a cross-tracks, following a track around to right, towards the centre of a wood. Continue through the wood to reach another cross-tracks. Turn right to reach a road and turn left to regain the start.

POINTS OF INTEREST:
Syderstone – This is an attractive village of flint cottages with a partly 12th-century church tower. Amy Robsart was born in the (now demolished) Syderstone Hall.
Barmer – This hamlet consists mainly of a farm and a church with a round tower on a pre-Christian site. Look out for an interesting inscription on one of the tombstones in the graveyard.

REFRESHMENTS:
The Lynn Arms, Syderstone.

Walk 44   BIRCHAM   5m (8km)

Maps: OS Sheets Landranger 132; Pathfinder 839.
A working windmill and three churches.
Start: At 767322, the King's Head Hotel, Great Bircham.

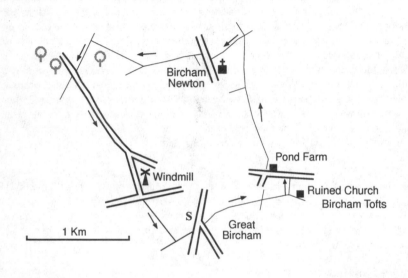

From the hotel, take the road opposite, signposted for West Rudham, but after 60 yards turn left along a broad track. Go ahead at a cross-tracks, continuing to reach a metalled road. Turn left, noting the ruined church of Bircham Tofts on the right.

Turn left at a road junction and, opposite Cuckoo Hill Lane, turn right along a grassy track to left of Pond Farm, soon joining a broader track from the farm. Where the track turns left after about $^2/_3$ mile, continue ahead along a path, walking with a hedge on your right. When the field ends, turn left along a broad track, following it to a road. Bircham Newton church is just to the left here.

Turn right along the road and, after 100 yards, turn left along a minor road. Where this road bears left, continue ahead along a stony track to reach a track fork. Take the larger track to right, continuing uphill to where the track ends, shortly after passing a wood on the left. Turn left along a field edge, walking with a hedge on your right, to reach a road. Turn left along the road and, after $^1/_2$ mile, turn right along a minor road. Go past **Bircham windmill**, on your left, and, at a road junction, continue ahead along a stony track. Follow the track to reach a junction of tracks and turn left to reach a road. Turn left again to reach **Great Bircham** and the start.

POINTS OF INTEREST:

Bircham Windmill – This restored, working windmill is open to the public.
Great Bircham – Bircham has three churches: the parish church is at Great Bircham, but the walk also passes the ruined church at Bircham Tofts and the small church at Bircham Newton.

REFRESHMENTS:

King's Head Hotel, Great Bircham.
When it is open, refreshments are also available at Bircham windmill.

Walk 45   **SWAFFHAM**   5$\frac{1}{4}$m (8$\frac{1}{2}$km)

Maps: OS Sheets Landranger 144 and 132; Pathfinder 901 and 881.

Breckland, a market town, woods and ancient tracks.

Start: At 818093, the car park, Station Street, Swaffham.

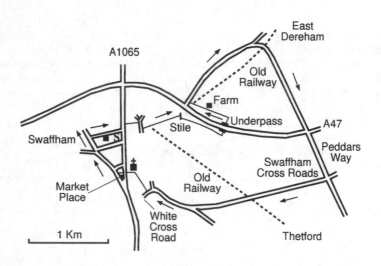

Return to the A1065, Fakenham road and turn left along it. Soon turn right at a waymarker post by a petrol station. Turn right at New Sporle Road, and, at a bend in the road, turn left over a stile. The path beyond ascends the bank of an old railway and then bears left, continuing through trees before descending to a stile. Cross and turn right, but soon, turn left along a bridleway.

Follow the bridleway as it nears the bypass, and, where it turns left, go through the underpass. Go along a track and turn left past a farmhouse to reach a road. Turn right and follow the road for $\frac{3}{4}$ mile to reach a road junction. Turn right, following Peddars Way to the A47. Cross, with care, and continue ahead to reach a crossroads of green lanes (the Swaffham Cross Roads). Turn right, crossing the **old railway line**, to reach a road junction.

Turn right, and then left down White Cross Road. Soon, turn right between railings to go along a footpath, following it across camping land to reach the **church**. Go through the churchyard to reach **Swaffham Market Place**. Cross the road and bear right to follow the road to a small car park. Turn left there and follow a road to a junction. Continue ahead down a minor road (Lynn Street and West Acre Road) and, after the railway bridge, turn right down Bears Lane to reach the A1065. Turn right and then right again to return to the car park.

POINTS OF INTEREST:
Old railway line – The dismantled line was once the King's Lynn to Dereham railway.
Church – The fine Parish Church of St Peter and St Paul was built in the period 1454-1490.
Swaffham Market Place – The Market Place dates from the reign of King John, though it now has some fine Georgian buildings, including the Butter Cross and Corn Exchange.

REFRESHMENTS:
The Norfolk Hero Inn, near the car park on the A1065.
There are numerous other options in Swaffham, particularly around the Market Place.

Walk 46　　　　　　　**BELAUGH**　　　　　　　5¹/₂m (9km)

Maps: OS Sheets Landranger 134, Pathfinder 862 and 883.

Broadland riverside walk through pretty villages.

Start: At 302188, the Bure Valley railway car park, Hoveton.

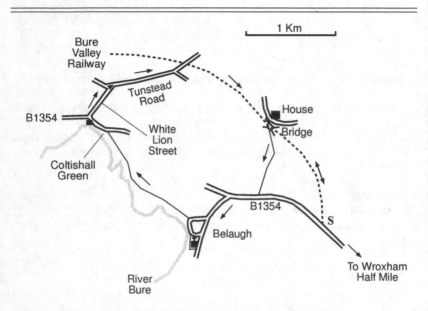

Go to the left of the station buildings, through a wicket gate and along a gravel and sand track running beside the miniature railway. Follow the track for a mile until, just after bridge No. 1283 (the first bridge you cross). There, turn left down steps and, at the bottom, pass between the railway and a thicket of trees into a field. Follow the field edge in a south-easterly direction keeping the hedge on your right. The path switches to the opposite side of the hedge after 200 yards: after a further 200 yards, turn half-right across the field corner to reach a small gap in the hedge line. Go through the gap and walk with a hedge on your left to reach a road. Turn right and, after 300 yards, turn left along a minor road signposted for Belaugh. Please take care: this road is busy, it is suggested that you walk on the left side as the bend at the Belaugh turn is blind.

Continue along the minor road to **Belaugh** village. Ignore two metalled roads off to the right and, about 100 yards after the metalled road signposted 'To River', turn right along a grassy track (Church Lane), following it to the church. The churchyard is a good spot to sit down and contemplate the river valley. The river here is in its meandering, 'senile' stage.

Leave through the gate at the far side of churchyard and continue downhill along a grassy track to reach a metalled road at the Old Rectory. Continue downhill along this minor road, passing the Broads Authority car (and boat!) park. When the minor road swings sharply right, uphill, cross the stile ahead into a field. Please keep dogs on leads here. Cross the field to a second stile on to a wide mown-grass track, walking ahead to enter a field. Walk with a hedge on your right and the river away to your left: this section of the walk can be soggy, but the cattle are used to walkers!

Ignore the first stile in the hedge on the right, but cross the stile/gate by a wooden cattle crush where the field narrows near houses. Now go ahead along a minor road to reach Coltishall green. At the green, cross the main road, with care, into White Lion Street (signposted for Tunstead). Follow the street to a grass triangle and bear right there into Tunstead Road. Follow this for $^3/_4$ mile to reach a bridge over the railway. Just before this bridge, turn left down steps to reach the **Bure Valley Railway** path. Turn right and follow the path for $1^3/_4$ miles to return to Hoveton station.

POINTS OF INTEREST:
Belaugh – Belaugh (pronounced Beela) was a favourite spot of Sir John Betjeman. The church has an interesting apostle screen.
Bure Valley Railway – The narrow gauge railway was opened by the musician, author and train buff Miles Kington in 1990. Passengers and staff are always friendly so keep one hand free for waving.

REFRESHMENTS:
There is a wide choice in Hoveton, Wroxham and Coltishall.

Walk 47   **HOW HILL**   5¹/₂m (9km)

Maps: OS Sheets Landranger 134; Pathfinder 883.
Broadland at its best.
Start: At 373191, the car park at How Hill.

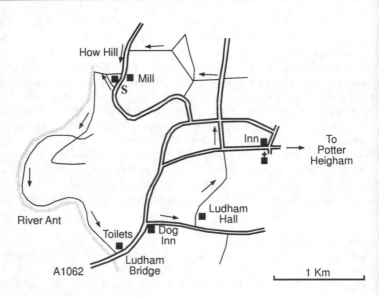

To reach the start, follow the brown tourist road signs from Ludham.

From the car park, follow the path to **How Hill** house. Take the path on the far side of the house towards the river. It is worth a short diversion here to visit Toad Cottage – an eel catcher's house, now renovated as the Broadland Life Museum.

Turn left at the river bank and follow it for 2 miles to Ludham Bridge, ignoring all tracks heading inland to your left. At the bridge, turn left, leaving the river, and following the pavement, with care, towards Ludham.

At the Dog Inn, cross the road, with even greater care, and follow the minor road signposted for Hall Common. After 600 yards, turn left up a farm drive to Ludham Hall. Follow the farm track, keeping the Hall on your right to reach a

T-junction. Turn left to reach a road. Cross this and continue ahead up a minor road opposite, following it for 900 yards and ignoring all roads off to both left and right. Now turn left along a footpath, crossing a field with a hedge on your right.

At the far side of the field, turn right along a bridleway, staying with it as it bends left, then right to reach a road. Turn left, downhill, to return to the car park and the start.

POINTS OF INTEREST:

How Hill – The site is run by a naturalist trust. It is open to the public, but you should check the opening times. The estate is actively managed to encourage the wildlife typical of Broadland, especially Swallowtail butterflies. There are nature trails to follow and, at weekends, the possibility of taking to the water on *The Electric Eel*, an electrically powered boat, ideal for peaceful viewing of wild creatures. The Broads Authority is campaigning for more holiday craft to use this clean, quiet form of energy.

The fine, thatched house was built at the end of the 19th century by a Mr Boardman, a first-class Norwich architect. Sadly, it is restricted to private parties engaged in conservation studies etc. The grounds are worth a visit for their azaleas.

The name How Hill is derived from the Norse for 'high place'.

REFRESHMENTS:

The Dog Inn, Ludham Bridge.
There are also numerous opportunities in Ludham.

Walk 48   **BRESSINGHAM** $5^1/_2$m ($8^1/_4$km)

Maps: OS Sheets Landranger 144; Pathfinder 944.

Slightly undulating countryside near the River Waveney (the boundary between Norfolk and Suffolk).

Start: At 083814, near the Post Office and Chapel, Bressingham.

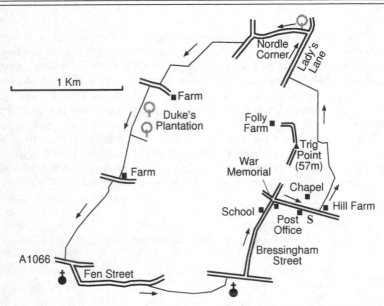

There is limited parking in Bressingham Street: please park with consideration.

From the Post Office, walk past the Methodist Chapel and turn left on to a footpath signed with a Norfolk County Council waymarker. Follow this grass path, with a garden on the left and a ditch on the right, to reach a plank bridge. Turn right, crossing the bridge and a stile. Turn half-left across the field beyond, heading towards a signpost. There, bear left across the same field to reach a stile. Cross and go to the left of a pond to reach a stile into the next field. Follow waymarkers across this field and over a plank bridge. Turn left, still following waymarkers, around the left edge of the field beyond, turning right at the end of the hedge.

Maintain direction across the next field, turning left along the far fence to reach a minor road (Lady's Lane). Turn right along the road, then left along a road signposted for Nordle Corner, passing a white house on the right. Turn left at the next road junction (signposted for Algar Road and Nordle Corner), then, after about 100 yards, turn right through a white gate and follow a signed footpath along the right-hand side of two fields to reach a stile. Cross this and a plank bridge, and head diagonally across the field beyond to its left corner. Cross a further plank bridge and follow the left-hand edge of the field beyond to reach an oak tree on the left. Turn left, and then right along the field edge to reach a signpost. There, turn left, following a row of trees to a road. Turn right for 100 yards, then left along a signed bridleway. Walk with a ditch on your left, passing Duke's Plantation. At the end of the ditch, turn left, and immediately right to resume your original direction across a field to reach a road.

Turn right, but soon go left over a signed footbridge and follow the right edge of a field to a plank bridge. Cross and go along the left side of the next field. Cross a track and continue down the field edge opposite, with a stream on your left to reach the A1066. Cross, with care, and turn left. Turn first right along a road signposted for Fen Street. Walk past a waymarker for Angles Way, a chapel on the right, and Oak Tree Farm, also on the right. Bear left with the road (and an Angles Waymarker) towards a white house. Go past Fen Farm, on the right, and head towards a church. When the road bends left, go straight ahead (Angles Waymarker) through a white gate and follow a track to a track junction. Continue ahead, passing a house on the left. If the track is very muddy, cross a plank bridge on the left after the house and continue towards the church. At the church, turn left up a road (Angles Waymarker) to reach the A1066 again. Turn right, with care, along the verge, passing the church, then cross the road, with even greater care, at a restaurant, and turn left up the minor road to **Bressingham**, with a nursery on your right. Walk past 'The Spinney' on your left and continue to a T-junction. Turn right into Fersfield Road to return to the Post Office.

POINTS OF INTEREST:
Bressingham – The Tudor, gabled red-brick Rectory is by Teulon who also designed Shadwell Park near Brettenham and some buildings at Sandringham.

REFRESHMENTS:
The Old Garden House Restaurant on the A1066 near Bressingham church.

Walk 49 LYNG 5¹/₂m (9km)

Maps: OS Sheets Landranger 133; Pathfinder 882.

A walk with views of the Wensum Valley, showing a wide variety of leisure uses of the countryside.

Start: At 069178, the Fox and Hounds Inn, The Street, Lyng.

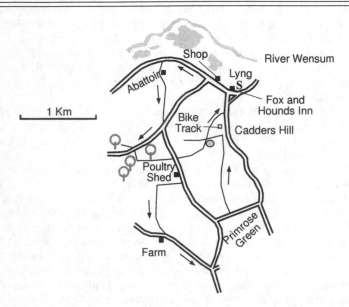

From the inn, turn right along The Street towards Elsing and Dereham. Go past the village stores on your right and ignore a minor road to the left. You are now walking parallel to the River Wensum away to your right. Now, about 100 yards after the de-restriction sign, turn left along a concrete road to an abattoir.

Go between the buildings and continue uphill along a green lane. Follow the lane to reach a road at the top of the hill. Turn right to reach a road fork. Take the right branch and go past houses on your right. About 50 yards after a wood begins on your right, turn left along a clear path going southwards through the wood. Towards the far side of wood follow the path as it veers left, still within the trees.

Follow the path as it leaves the wood, walking with a wire fence on your left to reach a road. Turn right, go past a chicken unit on your right, and then turn right along a footpath, walking with a hedge on your right. At the end of the field, turn left along a green lane.

Follow the track as it bends left and then continues to reach a road beyond a wooden barrier. Turn left to reach a T-junction. Turn left along a road signposted for Lyng, then take the first turn right (signposted for Primrose Green). After 200 yards, turn left along an enclosed bridleway, following it to a T-junction. (There is a motorbike track ahead on **Cadders Hill** here.)

Turn left along a sandy bridleway, but, after 200 yards, opposite a fishing pond, turn right over a stile into the bike arena. Now keep a wire fence on your left and motorbikes, and the hill, on your right and continue towards the village.

At the far side of the bike arena, turn right at a waymarker post and continue to a stile and double black gates. Cross the stile on to a road. Turn left to return to the village and starting point.

POINTS OF INTEREST:

Cadders Hill – The hill is used for motorbike scrambling events. As a result, this part of the walk can be rather noisy at times!

River Wensum – The Wensum Valley covered by the walk has large deposits of sand and gravels laid down by the river. These have been extracted for building purposes leaving the large pits filled with water. Several of these manmade lakes are private fisheries. Members of fishing clubs are given a quota of catches for each season.

The area is also home to many horses. In summer their fields are often embellished with tall, yellow-flowered plants. These are ragwort, an introduced species. In the 19th century, these were kept in selected botanic gardens. Their seeds escaped and were spread by the railways - seeds being wafted along the tracksides by the draught of passing locomotives. Pretty as it is – it is also food for the cinnabar moth caterpillar – it is deadly to livestock, leading to liver failure. Livestock avoid eating it if possible – hence it stands tall when all the grass around has been cropped. It is often a sign of too many beasts on too little grazing area.

REFRESHMENTS:

The Fox and Hounds, Lyng.

Walk 50   **NORTH CREAKE** $5\frac{1}{2}$m (9km)
Maps: OS Sheets Landranger 132; Pathfinder 840.
A ruined Abbey and farmland with good views.
Start: At 854382, the Jolly Farmers Inn, North Creake.

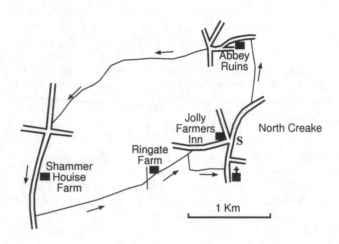

From the inn go along Wells Road, opposite, and, just before the road bears right after about ¹/₄ mile, bear left along a grassy path between hedges. On reaching a broad track by a white house, turn left, passing the ruins of **North Creake Abbey** on your left. Although the ruins are owned by English Heritage there is no entrance charge.

Continue along the metalled road, ignoring turnings to the left to reach a road junction. Cross and continue along the stony track ahead. Go past the barns and continue ahead, passing a track coming in from the left. The track bears left and eventually joins a road: continue ahead to reach a crossroads close to a farm. Go straight across, continuing along the road opposite. Go past the farm buildings of Shammer House Farm, on the left and, at the bottom of the hill, just before reaching some sheds on the right, turn left along a stony track, going past a pond.

When the track becomes a green path, continue ahead. Soon the path becomes broader and goes past a farm on the left – Ringate Farm. Now, just before reaching a telegraph pole – shortly before some houses – turn right through a hedge gap and go along a broad track. Follow the track as it bears around to the left, then go through a hedge gap and walk along the left side of the field beyond. Where the hedge ends, continue across the field, heading towards a building just to the left of North Creake Church. At the field's end, go through a hedge gap and bear diagonally right, aiming to the right side of the village hall. Turn left to reach a road and then left again to return to the start.

POINTS OF INTEREST:
North Creake Abbey – The abbey was founded in the 12th century as a hospital and almshouses but became an Augustinian Priory in 1206. In 1484 it was largely destroyed by fire and, in 1506, it was dissolved following the death of the monks, probably from plague.

REFRESHMENTS.
The Jolly Farmers Inn, North Creake,
There is also a teashop at the old forge and smithy.

Walk 51   BANHAM   5³/₄m (9km)

Maps: OS Sheets 144; Pathfinder 944.
A mixture of fen, pasture and arable farming.
Start: At 064882, Banham Church.

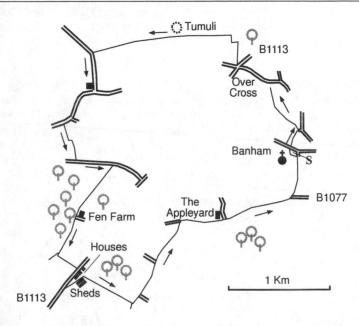

Parking is possible near the village green (near the church) or near the village hall. Please park considerately.

From the church, follow the path between Alexandra House (on the left) and a half-timbered house, going between gardens and then bearing right along a grass path between fields. At the path's end, by a footpath sign, turn left through a gate and follow the right edge of the field beyond to a gap, on the right, into the next field. Follow the right edge, then go through a barrier, over a plank bridge, and follow the right edge of the next field. Cross a plank bridge and again follow the right edge of a field. At the corner, go through tall grass and cross a last plank bridge. Cross a fence and follow the right edge of a field to a gate. Go through on to a road and turn left to reach a junction at Over Cross. Cross and go along a path to the left of a black shed, following it between fields. At its end, turn left along the top headland, and then right around a corner. Turn left at the next corner (you are now heading west) and walk with a hedge on your right. There are some small tumuli to the right, but these appear to have been ploughed almost level. Maintain direction along field edges to reach a minor road. Turn left down the road towards some buildings on the right at a junction. Turn right and go around left and right bends. About 100 yards after a farm track on the left (at the second bend) turn left along the right side of a hedge. When the hedge ends, go left, then right, around field edge and, at the next corner, maintain direction across the field to reach a road. Turn left – the track ahead leads into Great Fen.

Opposite a farm drive on the left, turn right and walk with a hedge on your left, crossing a field and continuing between a wood and fen, on the right, and the hedge. **Quidenham Hall** is on the right behind the trees. Just after the buildings of Fen Farm, on the left, maintain direction into a field, following its right edge toward houses. At the field's end, turn left along a track toward the houses. Turn right, with care, along a road (the B1113), turning sharp left after 300 yards. Go to the left of a long shed, walking with a fence on your left. At the end of the shed on your right, turn right along a field edge, now with a hedge on your right. At the field's end go between barns and around a pond on the left. Walk to the left of a flint building, and go down a track, passing further sheds on the left. You will see Banham Zoo on the right as you approach the village: the entrance is in the village. Continue down a track between trees and turn right along the road into Banham. Opposite the Zoo entrance, on the right before Grove Road, you will find The Appleyard on your left. Continue down the road, using the footpath on the left. Turn left down Crown Street, passing the Red Lion on the right, and turn left to return to the church.

POINTS OF INTEREST:

Quidenham Hall – This Elizabethan mansion with Georgian additions is now a Carmelite Nunnery.

The Appleyard – There are a coffee shop and toilets here, as well as Banham Cider, which can be sampled and purchased. Cider has been made here since the 13th century. It is made with local apples, and you can see the press in action between August and December.

REFRESHMENTS:

The Red Lion Inn, Banham.
The Appleyard coffee shop, Banham.

MANNINGTON HALL 6m (9¹/₂km)
or 9¹/₂m (15km)

Maps: OS Sheets Landranger 133; Pathfinder 841.
Peaceful farmland with delightful bluebell woods, moated
Manor House with rose gardens.
Start: At 141321, the car park at Mannington Hall.

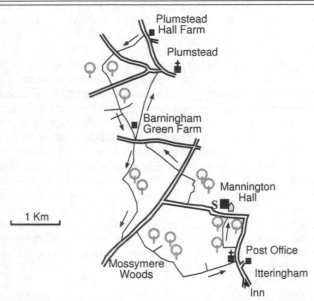

Return to the road, turn right for 400 yards, then turn right down a farm track, heading towards a small wood. At the wood, turn right along a track, with the wood on your left, following it as it swings around the wood and descends to a stream and a second wood. Turn left, then right after 20 yards and cross an earth bridge. Turn left and follow the left edge of a field to a road. Cross and continue along a bridleway with a hedge on your right. In the third field, follow the hedge on your left, continuing into a farmyard. Turn right just after the barn to reach a road. Turn left along the road for 200 yards to reach Barningham Green, on the right.

The longer route detours right from here making a circular route before rejoining the shorter route, which turns left here.

The longer route turns right. Ignore a track to left after 100 yards, continuing along a green track to reach a road at Plumstead. Turn right to a T-junction. Turn left (there is a Circular Walk sign here, as well as signposts for Holt and Baconsthorpe), walk through the village and continue to Plumstead Hall Farm. There, turn left along a bridleway, following it to a road. Cross and continue along a bridleway, heading downhill through woods. At the bottom of the hill, in a clearing, turn left and walk to a road. Cross and continue ahead along a wide track with a wood on your left, ignoring tracks off to both left and right. Follow the track as it leaves the woods, later passing a cottage on your left. At a junction of tracks, turn right to a road, rejoining the shorter route.

Cross the road and continue ahead, going uphill with a hedge on your left. Beyond the hill crest, continue with a hedge on your left, following the path as it swings right, then left, to enter scrubby trees with a stream to the right. Continue along the path to reach a road. Turn left and walk downhill (take care, this is a busy road) for 500 yards. Now, just before a wood on the right, turn right down a track. Cross a stile by a gate and walk ahead into **Mossymere Wood**. Continue through a clearing into old woods and follow a distinct path marked by white marks, ignoring all paths to both left and right as you walk uphill. Leave the wood over a stile and continue through wetland. The path later becomes a wide gravel track: follow this, ignoring a track to the left, to reach a road at Itteringham Church. Turn left (there is an inn 500 yards to the right), then, after 100 yards, turn left at a footpath sign opposite some council houses. Follow the path across a field and into a wood. Turn right and walk through the wood, ignoring all side paths. Leave the wood over a stile into a field and follow the left field edge to a gate/stile. Go through/over and turn left along the road beyond to return to **Mannington Hall** and the car park.

POINTS OF INTEREST:
Mannington Hall – A moated manor house built from 1460 by the Lumner family. The present owners, the Walpole family, have developed the estate with conservation in mind. Guided walks and other educational events are laid on, including 'Dawn Chorus' walks. Please note that the paths on the Walpole estate are permissive: dogs on leads please.
Mossymere Woods – The wood is delightful when the bluebells are out and the cuckoos return.

REFRESHMENTS:
There is a café at the Mannington Hall car park and an inn just off the route in Itteringham.

Walk 54   TRUNCH   6m (9¹/₂km)

Maps: OS Sheets Landranger 133; Pathfinder 842.

A pleasant waymarked farmland walk, with an interesting village.

Start: At 286351, Trunch Social Club car park, Brewery Road.

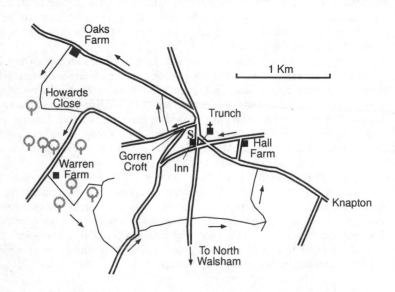

This route is a waymarked walk set up by the county and parish councils: see the information board at the start. Information leaflets may be bought at the village shops. Please note that some of the route is on 'white roads' not rights of way as marked on the Pathfinder map.

The car park is situated at the northern end of village. From it, turn left down Brewery Road and, opposite Gorren Croft, turn right along a footpath signed as part of the Circular Walk. Walk with a hedge on your right to reach a minor road. Turn left and follow the road for ³/₄ mile to reach a group of houses. Just after the last house (Oaks Farm), turn left along an enclosed bridleway, following it to a copse. There, at a T-junction of tracks, turn left along a farm track and follow it to a minor road at Howards Close.

Turn right along the road for 800 yards. At the bottom of a hill, turn left along a concrete drive in front of brick/flint cottage (Warren Farm) – look for the CW sign. Go through a kissing gate to reach an enclosed footpath and follow it through a wood. Beyond this, the path swings left, then right to reach a T-junction of paths. Turn right and follow a path for 1000 yards to reach a minor road. Turn left, but as the road swings sharp left, continue ahead, going uphill along an enclosed footpath to meet busy Trunch – North Walsham road.

Cross, with care, turn left for 5 yards, then go right along a footpath with a CW sign, keeping a hedge on your right and heading for the cream water tower and **radio masts** in the far distance. The footpath eventually meets a bridleway after 1000 yards: turn left along the bridleway and follow it to a road. Turn left, then right along a road signposted for **Hall Farm**. At a T-junction, turn left into **Trunch**, soon reaching a crossroads by the church. Turn right, then right again at the next junction to return to the car park.

POINTS OF INTEREST:
Radio Masts – The masts mark Bacton Natural Gas Terminal. Here gas from the southern North Sea gas fields is pumped ashore, cleaned and dried, and then has the classic gas odour added before being piped to your gas cooker. Most offshore operations are automated and operated from onshore - hence the radio towers.
Hall Farm – This fine, thatched 17th-century Hall Farm is worth a look – though this must be over the gate as it is private.
Trunch – The village church has a splendid font canopy.

The white building in the distance as you re-enter Trunch is Mundesley Hospital – a former tuberculosis sanatorium.

REFRESHMENTS:
There is an inn, *The Crown*, at Trunch.

Walk 55   **HORSFORD**   6m (9$\frac{1}{2}$km)

Maps: OS Sheets Landranger 134; Pathfinder 882.
Pleasant woodland trails through conifers and heaths.
Start: At 185175, the Forestry Commission car park.

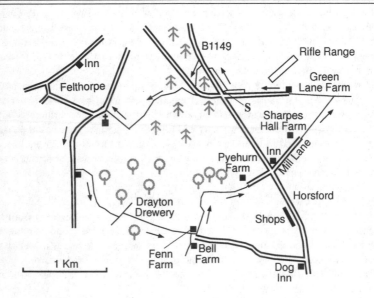

The car park lies beside the B1149 Norwich-Holt road, on the Holt side of Horsford village.

From the car park face away from the road and go through a wooden barrier. Turn left along a track, waymarked with blue and white arrows, which runs north-westwards parallel to the road. Now ignore the first track to the right (blue arrow), but where your track bends right (white arrow) leave it by continuing ahead into scrubland, going up a bank. Turn left, keeping conifers on your left, to reach a grey gate at the road. Go through and cross the road with care. Turn right, and as the road bends sharp right, turn left along a footpath through the trees. Follow the path to a road, cross and go along the bridleway opposite (to the right of the 'Keep Gateway

Clear' notice). Follow the bridleway as it swings left through the trees then leaves the main body of the wood. Continue to reach a T-junction of tracks. Turn right to reach a road and Felthorpe Church. Turn left along the road, following it for 1000 yards.

Just before Brands Farm, the first house on the left after Felthorpe, turn left over a stile (waymarked for the Circular Walk) on to a footpath into a garden. Keep to left side of the garden and watch out for the dog! Cross a stile into a field and follow its left edge. Cross a stile at the far side into **Drayton Drewery Wood**. Turn right along a clear track through the wood (with a field on your right) to reach a track junction. Turn left (there is a Circular Walk sign) and, after 50 yards, turn right along a path, continuing through the woods in your original direction. The path leaves the wood and heads downhill towards houses: at Fenn Farm, the first house on your left, turn left over a stile into a garden. Pass the house and outbuildings on your left and enter a field. Follow the right edge of the next three fields to reach a wood. Go through the right-hand corner of the wood on a clear path – there is an adventure centre on your right – and continue to reach a junction with a farm track at the far side of the wood. Turn right and follow the track, passing Pyehurn Farm on your left. Continue up Pyehurn Lane to the main road (B1149).

Cross, with care, and continue ahead along Mill Lane. The road becomes a green lane after **Sharpes Hall Farm**: continue along it to reach a T-junction, about $^{1}/_{2}$ mile after the farm. Turn left along a wide green track, following it to Green Lane Farm where the track becomes tarmac. Continue ahead and, just after a 'No Entry - Range' notice on your right, turn right along a path into Horsford Woods. At the next crossing ride, turn left to return to the car park.

POINTS OF INTEREST:
Drayton Drewery Wood – As you leave the wood look to your right. The new houses are Thorpe Marriott, a satellite town built since 1980 and named after William Marriott, the chief engineer of the local bit of The Midland and Great Northern Railway. The remains of the line have been opened as a long distance walk/ride/cycle way.
Sharpes Hall Farm – The sheep here are Texels. The owner is justly proud of them and has won several show prizes.

REFRESHMENTS:
There is an inn, *The Brickmakers*, at Horsford and other opportunities in Felthorpe, though these are a mile off route.

Walk 56   **DILHAM AND HONING**   6m (9¹/₂km)

Maps: OS Sheets Landranger 134; Pathfinder 862.

A tranquil Broadland walk, one for lovers of wide open skies.

Start: At 331252, the Village Hall car park, The Street, Dilham.

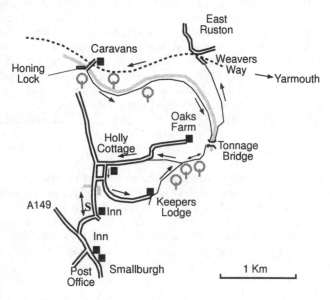

From the car park, turn left along The Street, passing Canal View and crossing a narrow bridge. Turn right along a minor road just after bridge and follow it to its end at Keepers Lodge (beware of geese!). Continue ahead along a bridleway, ignoring a track off to the right. The bridleway soon becomes a wide green lane: continue along it, watching for deer in the thicket on your right. At end of track, turn right to **Tonnage Bridge** - there is an information board here. Cross the bridge and a stile into a field, and turn left along the bank of the **canal**. Follow the canal over two further stiles, crossing the third field diagonally right to pick up a path along a dyke and a hedge. Now, keeping a hedge on your right to reach a wooden gate. Go through into East Ruston hamlet.

Continue ahead, up a gravel drive, with cottages on your right. Go through a second gate, then, after 5 yards, turn left along **Weavers Way**, which follows the bed of an old railway. Follow Weavers Way for 1 mile to the point where a gravel track crosses your path (there are caravans in the field on your right just before this point). Now turn left, off Weavers Way, on to this track, then, after 5 yards, turn right along a footpath signed by a waymarker post. Cross a plank bridge and then a wooden bridge over Honing Lock. Turn left and follow the canal back to Tonnage Bridge.

Reverse the outward route for 700 yards, then turn right off the track, at footpath finger post, into a field. Follow the left edge of the field, with a hedge on your left, then continue ahead in a second field. At the end of this field, at a footpath post, turn right to reach the road leading to Oak Farm. Turn left along the road towards Dilham. Just after Holly Cottage - the first house on your left - turn left. Walk to the end of this minor road and turn right. Now, at the main road through Dilham, turn left to return to the start: the inn is 20 yards down the road past the start.

POINTS OF INTEREST:

Tonnage Bridge – This was the spot where toll levies were collected. Walkers do not have to pay a toll to use the walk. In 1837 the fees were $\frac{1}{2}$d for each head of cattle, 3d per ton per mile for coal and 5d per ton per mile for wine.

Canal – The Dilham and North Walsham Canal was begun in 1824 to connect North Walsham with Yarmouth and the sea via the Broads river system. It joins the River Ant. The canal was never a raging success since it was relatively shallow - and is even more so today! Surprisingly the 9 mile stretch to North Walsham required six locks. The key to work the higher locks was collected from the lock-keepers cottage in Honing.

Weavers Way – The Way in this area uses an old railway trackbed closed in 1959, one of British Rail's earliest prunings.

REFRESHMENTS:

There is an inn, *The Cross Keys*, in Dilham, near the start of the walk.

Walk 57   **KNAPTON**   6m (9¹/₂km)

Maps: OS Sheets Landranger 133; Pathfinder 842.

Pleasant bridleways and tracks – a Community that cares.

Start: At 307342, St Peter and St Paul Church, The Street, Knapton.

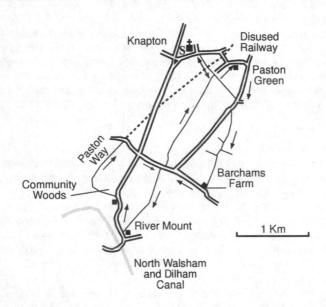

From the church, turn left, downhill, then turn right into Timber Loke (which has footpath signs). At the end of the Loke, follow a clear path across a field, then walk ahead with a hedge on your left. Go over a railway bridge to reach a junction of paths by a house.

Turn left here and go along a road to a T-junction. Turn right, then right again at the next junction. Now ignore a road off to the left, but where your road bends right, keep straight on up an overgrown green lane. There is no signpost, but the way is clear. Follow the lane to its end at **Barchams Farm**.

Turn right along a road to reach a junction. Continue ahead for 250 yards, then turn left along a footpath, crossing a field. Note that this is not quite as shown on the Pathfinder map. Follow the path along the left edge of several fields to reach a minor road at River Mount.

Turn right along the road and, just after a house on your left, turn left into **Community Woods**. Follow the mown path, with a hedge on your right, and, after passing a mature wood on your right, keep straight on to reach a finger post. Turn right along the **Paston Way**.

Follow the Paston Way – which later uses the old railway trackbed – but, just before a bridge, turn left up steps to a road. Turn right and follow the road to a junction. Continue ahead (signposted Bacton, but still on the Paston Way). After 500 yards, turn left along a bridleway, following it for 1 mile to reach a junction of three paths by a house.

Turn left and retrace the outward route back to the start.

POINTS OF INTEREST:

Barchams Farm – This is the original type of smallholding, the owners having many old breeds of poultry and cows.

Community Woods – The Wood is managed by a team of local residents headed by the (goat owning) Vicar. There are 57 acres which are being replanted with Oak, Ash, Beech and Hazel. The meadow is a riot of wild flowers and there are seats to sit and gaze at the lovely view of the valley stretching back to North Walsham. The real name of the wood is Pigneys Wood.

Paston Way – This pathway was recently devised by local councils and links North Walsham and Mundesley.

REFRESHMENTS:

None en route or in Knapton, but full facilities are available 3 miles away in either North Walsham or Mundesley.

Walk 58   HAPPISBURGH   6m (9¹/₂km)

Maps: OS Sheets Landranger 133; Pathfinder 842.
A bracing coastal walk.
Start: At 379312, Happisburgh Church.

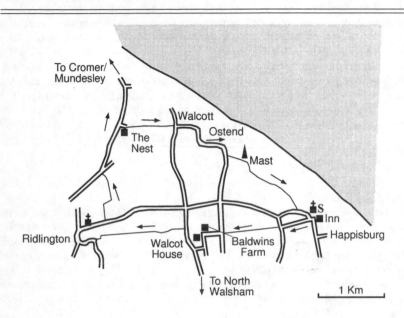

From the church, go downhill to the main road through the village. Turn right and, as the road bends sharp right, continue ahead along a footpath across a field. The footpath sign is hidden in the hedge, but the path is clear. Continue with a hedge on your right, following it to a barn. Pass the barn on your right to reach a road.

Cross and continue along the minor road opposite, following it as it swings sharp left at Baldwins Farm to reach a junction. Turn right to reach a T-junction. Turn right, with care – this road can be busy – for 300 yards, then turn left along a signed footpath, walking with a hedge on your right. At the end of the hedge cross the field and continue in the same direction, now with a hedge on your left. At the end of this hedge, continue along a clear path across the field until you are below a power line. There, at a waymarker, turn left and follow a hedge on your right as it swings right to reach a road at a telephone box in Ridlington Street.

Turn right along the road to a T-junction. Turn right, then fork right at the village sign and go past the church. (Note that the paths around Ridlington have been diverted and are not as shown on the OS maps.) At the 'Road Materials Store', turn left along a footpath, walking with a hedge on your left. About 20 yards after the hedge ends, turn right at a waymarker and walk to the next waymarker. There, turn left and follow a path which meets a track leading to some houses.

Pass a barn on your left and continue to a road. Turn left, then right along a road signposted for Bacton. Ignore a road off to right and, just after The Nest, turn right along a footpath, walking with a wall, and then a hedge, on your right. Follow the path eastwards to reach a road at the Walcot village sign. Go half-left across the road and continue along a minor road signposted Ostend/Coastline village.

Continue along the road as it bends right, left and then right again. About 100 yards after the final bend, turn left along a track leading to a mast. Just before the mast, turn right at a waymarker and go across a field. Go through a gap in a hedge and turn left, following the hedge, and then waymarkers on the cliff top path to return to **Happisburgh**.

POINTS OF INTEREST:

Happisburgh – The village's name is pronounced *Haysbro*. There has been a lighthouse here since 1791. It warns seamen of the Happisburgh Sands 8 miles offshore which have claimed many victims, some of them buried in the churchyard. It was also used as a beacon for First World War Zeppelins. They congregated overhead before setting off inland – navigation was not so hot in those days!

As with most old villages there is a local ghost tale. It is said that the headless figure of a smuggler, throttled by his mates in a dispute over loot, can be seen emerging from the village well.

REFRESHMENTS:

There is an inn, *The Hill House*, and a village store at Happisburgh.

Walk 59   TROWSE AND KIRBY BEDON   6m (9¹/₂km)

Maps: OS Sheets Landranger 134; Pathfinder 903.

Pleasant views of the Yare valley.

Start: At 269077, the picnic site, Whitlingham Lane, Trowse.

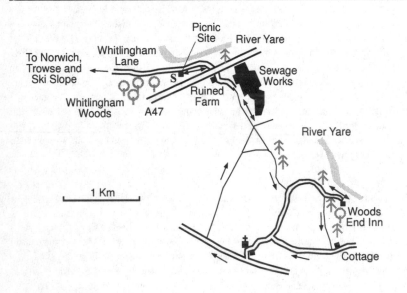

To reach the start, follow the signs to the Ski Club, then continue along the road.

From the picnic site, close to **Whitlingham Woods**, turn right and follow the road, passing houses and going under the A47/Norwich Southern Bypass. Continue past a ruined farm on your right to reach a T-junction by a Furniture Store. Turn left. The road later becomes concrete: continue along it, passing a **Sewage Works** and Laboratory on your left.

    Now, as the road swings sharp right, uphill, turn left through a green gate and turn right to follow a footpath going uphill across a field. Follow this clear path, which meets a track from the right just before reaching a copse, and pass the copse on your left. Continue downhill to reach a minor road.

Turn left and follow the road to Woods End Inn, Bramerton. Now retrace your steps along road, but, 10 yards after the Anglian Water compound on your right, turn left along a footpath, going uphill with a wood on your left. At the end of the wood, continue ahead along a clear path, passing a cottage on your left and continuing to reach a road.

Turn right and walk to a T-junction. Turn left, walking past Kirby Bedon Church and ruins to reach the main road. Turn right, downhill – please take care and use the pavement. Turn right at the entrance to the Sewage Works and follow the concrete track/bridleway to rejoin the outward route near the sewage works/laboratory. Now retrace the outward route under the bypass to return to the start.

POINTS OF INTEREST:

Whitlingham Woods – These are ancient woods as the Dogs Mercury growing here shows. The 60 acres of wooded escarpment are managed as a Country Park by the Council and a Wildlife Trust. The woods can be explored via a network of paths, some suitable for wheelchairs. The Ranger service also put on events. The area was used for flint mining and knapping (trimming to form tools) from Neolithic times until the 18th century. Tunnels were dug into the hillside – one of which contained a human skeleton! The chalk quarried was burnt in two lime kilns to produce lime for agriculture.

Sewage Works – Possibly one of the largest in Norfolk – but surprisingly (and relatively) odour free. In the days before Euro-hygiene the workers here were known to sell tomatoes grown on the sludge. Where did the seeds come from? The human digestive system clearly cannot cope with all vegetable matter!

REFRESHMENTS:

The Woods End Inn, Bramerton.

There are also full facilities in Norwich, just 2 miles away.

Those preferring a picnic should bring their own tomato sandwich!

Walk 60 MIDDLETON TOWERS AND EAST WINCH 6m (10km)

Maps: OS Sheets Landranger 132; Pathfinder 880.

An easy walk through mainly open countryside.

Start: At 667177, Middleton Towers.

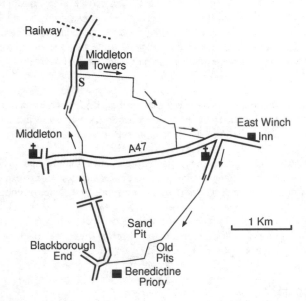

From the entrance to **Middleton Towers**, go eastwards along Tower Lane. The house and medieval gatehouse can soon be seen on the left. After $\frac{1}{2}$ mile the track bears right along a ditch, then slightly left, with a wood on the right. Where the field ends at the start of the wood on the left, turn left alongside the wood, and left again at the corner for 50 yards to reach the next hedge. Turn right past the first wooden barrier and cross a field diagonally, heading south-east towards the far corner of the first wood on the left. Pass close to the wood corner and maintain direction to reach the far left corner of the field, with another wood some way to the left. At the field corner, pass a wooden barrier to reach a broad track and turn left.

At a farm, bear right, then left with the track to reach a T-junction. Turn right along a track and, on reaching a bungalow on the right, turn left through a hedge gap and cross a field diagonally to the far corner, heading for first gap just to right of **East Winch** church, visible ahead. Go through the gap and continue ahead, now heading directly for the church tower. At the field end, cross the main road (the A47), with care, and turn left along a metalled footpath past the church. At the end of the churchyard, turn right along Church Lane. After $1/2$ mile, bear right with the road, ignoring a left fork. Where the metalled road ends at a large house on the right, continue ahead through a gateway and along the stony track beyond. Pass cottages on the right and, at the next house on the right, where the track goes left to a farm, continue ahead through a gate. Soon you pass a large sand pit on the right and overgrown sandpits on the left (now transformed into tree-lined lakes – pity about the litter). Continue along the track, ignoring a track on the left to pass a house on the left. Bear right with the track, passing a track on the left. Now continue ahead. The remains of a Benedictine nunnery can be seen a little to the left near the farm buildings.

On reaching a road just before some houses, turn right and, at a road junction after $1/2$ mile, go straight ahead along a gravel track. Middleton village can be seen to the left. Pass Mill Farm, cross the A47, again with care, and continue along the track opposite, with a hedge on your left and good views to the north and east. On reaching a track from the right, at the field end, turn left, then right to reach a road (Station Road). Turn right and follow the road back to the start.

POINTS OF INTEREST:
Middleton Towers – This is a picturesque house with a 14th-century gatehouse. It also boasts a railway station, although the line is now only used by traffic from the industrial sand workings nearby.
East Winch – The village has a modern, well-equipped RSPCA animal hospital which treats many sick seals rescued from the Norfolk coast.

REFRESHMENTS:
There are opportunities at both East Winch and Middleton, though in each case they are about $1/2$ mile off route.

Walk 61   COLTISHALL GREEN   6¹/₂m (10¹/₂km)

Maps: OS Sheets Landranger 134, Pathfinder 862 and 883.

A traditional farmland area in the Bure Valley.

Start: At 277196, the public car park by the Rising Sun Inn, Coltishall Green.

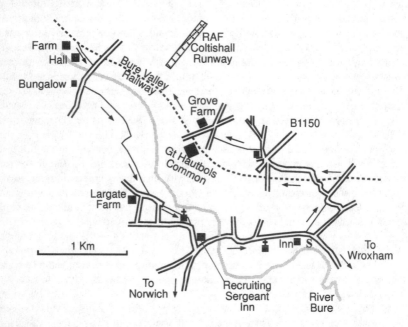

From the car park, cross the road to enter an enclosed footpath by a phone box. Follow the path across a field to reach a road. Continue ahead along the road, but just before a railway bridge crosses it, turn left up steps to reach a track beside the narrow gauge railway. Turn left.

Now just before road bridge No. 1297 crosses the railway, leave the track by turning left through a gap in the hedge to enter a field. Walk with a hedge and road on your right to the first telegraph pole, leaving the field on to a road and turning right. At the five cross ways, cross the main road (B1150), with care, and turn right into North Walsham Road. After passing the second set of semi-detached houses, turn left along a signed path across a small common. Maintain direction between two fields to reach a minor road near Grove Farm.

Turn right, then left along a minor road. Go under a railway bridge and immediately turn left on to Great Hautbois (pronounced Hobbis) Common. Keep the railway on your left and, after 30 yards, turn left up steps to reach the track again. Turn left and follow the track for $1^1/_2$ miles passing one end of RAF Coltishall's runway on the right. When the railway enters a farmyard, leave the track and turn left, keeping a dairy and Mayton Hall on your right. Follow the farm drive to a road and turn right. Follow the road over two streams and, 50 yards after the second bridge, at a bungalow, turn left along a signed path into a field. The footpath cuts diagonally across three fields but the path walked by local residents keeps to the left edge of the fields, with a hedge and the River Bure on your left: it is advisable to keep to field edge unless there is a well marked path across the field crops.

Once in the third field, turn right, with a fence on your right for 200 yards, then turn left and cross the field (crossing a stream via an earth bridge) to the fence on the far side. Turn left and cross a stile into a fourth field. Now continue in the original direction to reach a cattle pound at the far side. Cross the stile to the right of the pound on to a gravel track. Turn left and, at its end, go over a stile and bridge into a field. Follow a clear path across two fields, with the hedge and river 20 yards to your left, to enter a churchyard. Follow the path through the yard, with the church on your right, exit through a gate into Rectory Road. Turn left and follow the road to T-junction by the Recruiting Sergeant Inn. Turn left and follow the main road to the River Bure. Cross via the footbridge, leaving Horstead village to re-enter **Coltishall**.

At Coltishall island filling station cross the main road with care and turn right along High Street. Follow this past the church to return to the start.

POINTS OF INTEREST:

Coltishall – Kings College Cambridge is Lord of the Manor of Coltishall. From the 16th – 18th centuries, Coltishall was a thriving wherry port, wherries being flat-bottomed sailing barges. Today it is the highest navigable point on the Bure. The inns on the green are renowned watering points for hire craft. If you think you have problems parking a car, try watching the tourists park boats!

REFRESHMENTS:

There are several opportunities on the Green and in Coltishall and Horstead villages.

Walk 62   **ALDBOROUGH**   6½m (10½km)

Maps: OS Sheets Landranger 133; Pathfinder 841 and 842.

Sleepy villages linked by quiet lanes and tracks.

Start: At 186343, Aldborough Green.

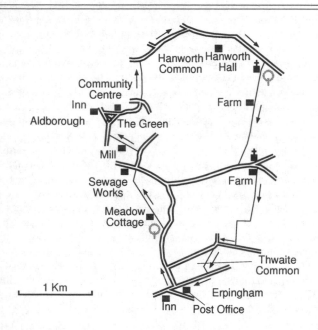

From the north-east corner of the Green, take the minor road to the right of the Community Centre, following it to a T-junction. Turn left, then, after 5 yards, turn right up a bridleway following it to a minor road. Turn right and follow the road to Hanworth Common, crossing a cattle grid. On the Common – which is grazed by cattle and sheep and is not the spot for a picnic unless you have sarnies for 25 bullocks! – turn right at the four cross-ways, following the road signed for Aylsham and Norwich, leaving both the Common and the village, and passing Hanworth Hall on your right just after a second cattle grid. At the top of the hill, turn right up a footpath, to left of the church, signed as part of the Weavers Way. After about 100 yards, bear left at a fork following Weavers Way along a wide track to a farmyard. Go through the farmyard and continue along a concrete track to meet a minor road.

Note that Weavers Way here and 1 mile further on does <u>not</u> follow the footpaths marked on the Pathfinder maps.

Turn left, then, opposite the church, turn right into the second road (signed 'Children's book centre') and, after 20 yards, turn right along Weavers Way into a farm. Go past barns on your right and continue ahead along a wide track between fields, following it for a mile to reach a road after passing between renovated farm buildings. Note that this is again not quite as shown on the map. Turn right with the Way, passing a riding school on your right. The road bends left and then, as it bends right again, turn half-left along a footpath, crossing a field corner to a stile. Go over on to a common, crossing it on a compass bearing of 210 degrees to reach a wooden gate, bridge and stile in the far hedge. Cross these into an enclosed footpath, following it over a second stile on to a road.

Turn right, passing the **Ark Restaurant** on your right, and continuing through **Erpingham** village. Take the next road on the right (Chapel Road) – or go straight on to reach the Spread Eagle Inn. Follow Chapel Road gently uphill and, at the far end of the wood on your left, turn left up a track signed for Meadow Cottage. Follow the track through two fields, then, just before the gate to a cottage, turn right over a stile into a field. Cross two fields, aiming towards a single bungalow to the right of a group of houses at the far side, 100 yards to the right of a sewage works, to reach a road. Cross and continue ahead up a minor road, passing Thwaite Hill farm on your right. As the road bends right, turn left along a footpath following the right edge of a field. Cross a wooden bridge into a garden and follow the path to a driveway. Bear right along the drive, going away from a converted mill, and, at its end, turn right along a road to return to **Aldborough** and the Green.

POINTS OF INTEREST:

The Ark – The restaurant obviously has free-range eggs on the menu.

Erpingham – The village was the home of Sir Thomas Erpingham who commanded the English archers at Agincourt. The family home was on a site opposite the Ark Restaurant.

Aldborough – This was a medieval market town - see the village sign on the Green. The village has a renowned 'big hitting' cricket team: you are advised to park towards the southern end of the Green in summer!

REFRESHMENTS:

The Spread Eagle Inn, Erpingham.

There are also opportunities in Aldborough, and at the Ark Restaurant passed on the route.

Walk 63   **INTWOOD**   6¹/₂m (10¹/₂km)

Maps: OS Sheets Landranger 134; Pathfinder 902.

A peaceful stroll along the Tas Valley.

Start: At 197042, Intwood Church.

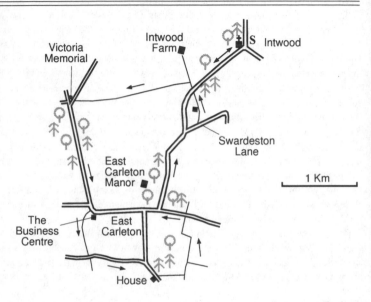

From the church, turn right along the road towards East Carleton. As the road bends left, at a ford sign, turn right up the drive to Intwood Farm, signed as part of the **Upper Tas Valley Walk**. After 50 yards, turn left through a gate (also signed for the Walk) and follow the track beyond to a road. Turn left, then left again (Hethersett Road) at the Victoria Monument. Continue along the road into East Carleton village. Now, ignore a road to the right and, at a sharp left bend, just before The Business Centre, turn right along a footpath.

After a further 200 yards the path bends left into a field: follow the hedge on your left southwards. At the end of the hedge, maintain direction along a clear track across a second field to reach a road. Turn left to reach a T-junction. Turn right and, opposite a house, turn left along a clear footpath through trees. Cross a bridge and a stile, and follow the clear path beyond across a field. Cross a wide wooden bridge and go up a bank to reach a horse paddock. Turn left and walk with the fence on your right and trees on your left. At the end of the paddock turn left over a stile (signed for the Upper Tas Walk) and cross the field beyond. Maintain direction, with a hedge on your right, and, at the end of the hedge, turn left along a wide track, heading downhill, again with a hedge on your right. Go through a gate and turn right (as signed for the Walk) to follow a clear path to a road.

Turn left, then take the first road to the right (Intwood Lane), following it past **East Carleton Manor** on your left. Take the next road on the right (**Swardeston Lane**), but just before the houses, turn left up a drive. About 10 yards before the end house, turn right through a gate signed for the Walk and immediately turn left, northwards, with the house and a hedge on your left. Cross a stile, a drive and another stile into a field. Cross the field, go over a wooden bridge and through a metal gate on to a road. Turn right to return to start.

POINTS OF INTEREST:

Upper Tas Valley Walk – This is a linear walk linking Norwich and New Buckenham. A route description is available from the local council.

East Carleton Manor – The Manor was built by Colin Chapman, the racing driver and founder of the Lotus International sports car firm. The house is built in the style of a colonial mansion in the southern USA.

Swardeston Lane – The village of Swardeston, just off the route, was the birthplace of the First World War nurse Edith Cavell who was shot for helping allied soldiers to escape from Brussels. As you tread these peaceful byways perhaps it is the time to ponder her last words: '*I must have no hatred or bitterness towards anyone*'.

REFRESHMENTS:

None on the route, but available at Mulbarton, a couple of miles to the south and, of course, at Norwich 3 miles north of the start.

Walk 64   BARNHAM BROOM   6½m (10½km)

Maps: OS Sheets Landranger 144; Pathfinder 902.

Peaceful byways between forgotten hamlets.

Start: At 086074, the car park at the Village Hall/playing fields, Norwich Road, Barnham Broom.

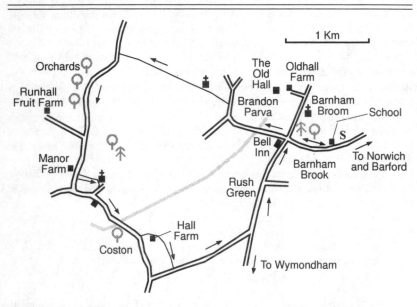

From the car park, head westwards along Norwich Road, passing the school to reach a crossroads. Go straight on down Mill Road and into Brandon Parva. At the next junction, bear right with the main road, then, after a further 200 yards, at the Agricultural Engineers, turn left up a drive signposted for the church.

Pass the church on your right and continue along a track going over a hill. At the end of the track, maintain direction, with a hedge on your left, to reach a road. Turn left. Go past a road to the right (a 'No Through Road' which leads to the Runhall Fruit Farm, where fruit is sold in season) and, after a further 500 yards, at the drive to Manor Farm, on the right – and just after sign for 'East Green' – turn left over an earth bridge into a field. Cross the field to reach a church hidden in the trees. Go through the churchyard, leaving it through the main gate on to a road.

Turn right, then take the first turn left, just before a thatched barn. Follow this winding road downhill and over a bridge into Coston. About 300 yards beyond the bridge, as the road bends sharp right, turn left up the drive to Hall Farm. Follow this tarmac drive past the house, on your right, then turn right, uphill, and pass barns on your left. Continue to reach a road.

Turn left to reach a T-junction. Turn left, downhill, ignoring a road to the right signposted for Carleton Forehoe. Continue along the road into **Barnham Broom**, passing the Bell Inn on your left to reach a crossroads. Turn right to return to the start.

POINTS OF INTEREST:

Barnham Broom – This is a sleepy little spot in the upper Yare Valley. On the walk you cross the Yare twice - just before Brandon Parva and just before Coston. The only danger time on these quiet roads with wide verges is, perhaps, on Saturday afternoons as the golf club complex north of the village is a favourite for wedding receptions! Also north of the village is the church and the Old Hall. The Hall is Tudor and built of red brick.

The plethora of parishes locally is an indication of the past wealth of this area. Norfolk is home to many 'lost' or 'reduced' villages. In medieval times the population of the area would have been much greater.

REFRESHMENTS:
The Bell Inn, Barnham Broom.

Walk 65 **PULHAM MARKET AND PULHAM ST MARY** $6\frac{1}{2}$m ($10\frac{1}{2}$km)
Maps: OS Sheets Landranger 156, Pathfinder 945 and 944.
Pretty lanes around two charming villages.
Start: At 198862, The Green, Pulham Market.

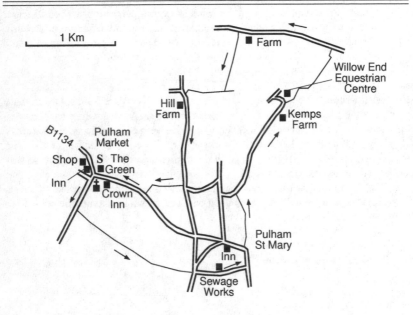

From The Green, **Pulham Market**, cross the main road (the B1134), with care, towards the church and turn right. Go past the Crown Inn and turn left towards Dickleburgh. About 100 yards after the de-restriction sign, turn left along an enclosed footpath to a field. In the field, turn right, then left and walk eastwards, with a stream on your right, to enter a small copse.

Turn right over a wooden bridge (taking care because of the holes), then turn left over a concrete bridge to resume your original direction, but with the stream now on your left. Follow the clear path through a meadow, eventually entering a green lane between the stream and the path of an old railway.

Follow the lane to a road. Cross diagonally left into the road opposite and go past a **sewage works** to reach a T-junction. Turn left to enter **Pulham St Mary**. Just after the road bends sharp left, turn right along a drive before the church. At the end of the drive, continue into a field and head northwards with a hedge on your left.

Cross a stile and the field beyond, heading towards a bungalow. Turn left and follow a hedge to a road. Turn right along the road and, at the top of the hill, pass Kemps Farm and a footpath on your right. Now, at the Willow End Equestrian Centre a little further on, turn right and cross a waymarked bridge. Turn left and follow the hedge on your left to reach a track. Turn right, and then left at a waymarker, and follow a hedge on the right to reach a road.

Turn left to reach a crossroads. Go straight over towards Bush Green and, after 600 yards, go past a farm on your left. After a further 100 yards, turn left along a footpath, following the hedge on your right for $1/2$ mile. At its end, go into the next field and turn right along a clear path, again walking with a hedge on the right, to reach a road.

Turn left, go past Hill Farm and continue to a point about 10 yards before a minor road to the left. There, turn right along a green lane, following it to a road (the B1134 again). Turn right to return to the start, using the pavement on the opposite side of the road for safety, but taking great care when crossing to reach it.

POINTS OF INTEREST:
Pulham Market - This was once known as Pulham St Mary Magdalene, the present name revealing that it was once a market town. Today it has been designated as a 'Conservation Area' by the Local Authority. This prevents unsuitable building works which might spoil the local character. The tall roof houses are typical of this part of South Norfolk and North Suffolk.

Sewage Works – Most local walks seem to include a sewage works - this one is sited in the aptly named Dirty Lane. For those who are interested, the clinker beds below the revolving arms hold beasties which devour the organic bits in raw sewage.

Pulham St Mary – The village has an interesting sign depicting an airship. These were stabled at an airfield south of the village and were known as 'The Pulham Pigs'.

REFRESHMENTS:
The Crown Inn, Pulham Market.
There is also an inn and a shop just off route in Pulham St Mary.

Walk 66   **WALSINGHAM** $6\frac{1}{4}$m (10km)

Maps: OS Sheets Landranger 132; Pathfinder 840.
Historic shrines on a famous pilgrims' route.
Start: At 916337, East Barsham Church.

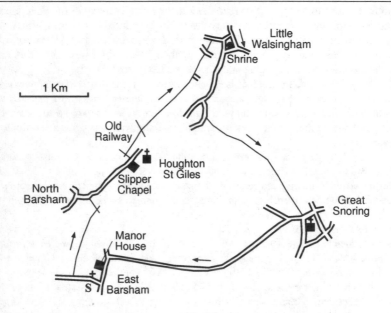

From the church take the West Barsham road (with the church on your right) and, after about 300 yards – and opposite a brick wall on the left – take a narrow path to the right, ascending the bank and continuing along the old railway track. Follow the track for just over $\frac{1}{2}$ mile, then, shortly after emerging from a cutting and passing under power lines, turn left through a gap and turn right along a field edge.

Follow the path around the side of the field and, on reaching the hedge gap opposite, turn right, then right again. Bear left over a footbridge to reach a road at North Barsham. Turn right along the road for $\frac{1}{2}$ mile and, just after passing **Slipper Chapel** on the right, turn left along a concrete track. After 60 yards turn right to rejoin the old railway track. At the next bridge, turn left down steps, rejoining the track by way of the steps opposite. Continue ahead at a cross-tracks, passing some station buildings and an Orthodox chapel on the right. Now continue ahead along a metalled road to reach a T-junction by the Wells and Walsingham Railway sign.

Turn right along the road and right again at a junction. On reaching the Anglican shrine on the right, turn right to reach the **Little Walsingham** village square and then left down the main street, with the Abbey ruins on your left. Where the road forks, bear left, following the sign for East Barsham. Now, where the road bears right at a house, bear left along a stony track. Where the main track bears left, continue ahead along a narrow path between hedges to reach a road.

Turn right (or to see the picturesquely named village of Great Snoring, turn left and take the next three right turns to arrive back at same point). Follow the road for about $1^1/_2$ miles to reach the main road, turning left there to return to the start. En route, note the attractive 16th-century manor house and adjoining Toad Hall, on the right.

POINTS OF INTEREST:

Slipper Chapel – The 14th-century Slipper Chapel at Houghton St Giles is now a Catholic shrine. It was the last stopping place for pilgrims who removed their shoes here (hence the name) before walking the last mile to Walsingham.

Little Walsingham – The village has been a focal point for pilgrims for 900 years and is visited by 100,000 people every year. Notable buildings include the Abbey ruins (originally the medieval Priory) and the modern Anglican shrine.

REFRESHMENTS:

There are numerous opportunities at Little Walsingham and an inn at East Barsham.

Maps: OS Sheets Landranger 133; Pathfinder 842.
Pretty flint hamlets linked by tracks, and a tale to tell.
Start: At 243393, the Village Hall car park, Northrepps.

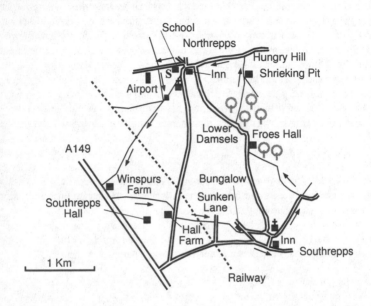

From car park, turn left along the road towards Cromer. After 300 yards turn left down an enclosed bridleway, with **Northrepps Airfield** on your right. Follow the bridleway to a house. Turn right, but, after 20 yards, bear half-left across a field (look for the Circular Walk sign) to reach the railway. Cross, with great care, and continue in your original direction across a large field, aiming towards farm buildings on the skyline. When the path meets a hedge, keep this on your right, following it into the farmyard of Winspurs Farm. Exit the farmyard on to the A149 and turn left, with care. After 200 yards, turn left along a bridleway, following it along the right edge of two fields to reach a road. Turn right and, after 300 yards, opposite the white rails at Hall Farm/Iceni Anglia, turn left along a footpath, crossing a field - aim for the church tower: the crossing point is marked by a white rail - to reach the railway again.

Cross, with care, and continue in your original direction over a field, a sunken lane and two further small fields. In the fourth field, bear half-right towards the right side of bungalow opposite, exiting the field with the bungalow on your left and a chicken run on your right. Go down steps and along a drive to Sandy Lane. Turn right to a road junction. Turn left (signposted for Mundesley) and, at the next road junction, turn left (signposted for Northrepps) towards **Southrepps Church**. At the road junction by the church, turn right (signed for the Circular Walk), and follow the road for 800 yards to where it turns sharp right. There, turn left up a wide green track, following it as it swings past a wood to reach a road at Frogshall Farm. Leave the Circular Walk here, turning right along the road. Follow the road as it swings sharply left, then right, then left again.

Just after 'Lower Damsels' (lovely name, lovely spot), turn right, uphill, on a footpath through a wooden gate, walking with a wood on your right. At the top of the rise go ahead through young deciduous trees and cross a stile. Continue ahead along an enclosed track, ignoring a path to the left to reach a T-junction of tracks. Turn left and walk to a road at Hungry Hill. The large pond in the copse on your right is known as **Shrieking Pit**. Turn left and follow the road into **Northrepps** village. Go past the turkey works on your right and the inn on your left, then ignore the first road to left, taking the next (at the village sign, signposted for Cromer) to pass the school and regain the start.

POINTS OF INTEREST:

Northrepps Airport – Concorde rarely lands here, but it is quite good fun at weekends and on the annual airshow day.

Southrepps Church – This is well worth a visit. Its size points to the prosperity of the village in times past.

Northrepps – The village has some interesting buildings, particularly the thatched houses by the village sign. The flint facing to many cottages is typical of the area.

Shrieking Pit – Legend has it that, in the 18th century, a local lass fell victim to forbidden love. In her sorrow she took to roaming the local tracks. One dark night she fell (or jumped) into the pond here and, proverbially, 'went down three times but re-appeared only twice'. Each time she slipped beneath the icy waves she let out a piercing, ghastly shriek. Her soul, even today, cannot rest in peace for, it is said, that 'disturbances' occur on the night of February 24th. You are a down-to-earth walker and do not believe such tosh... do you?

REFRESHMENTS:
There are good inns at both Northrepps and Southrepps.

Walks 68 & 69 REEPHAM, SALLE AND HEYDON 7m (11km)
or 11m (17½km)

Maps: OS Sheets Landranger 133; Pathfinder 861.
Prosperous farmland and a village with a film star history.
Start: At 101228, Reepham Market Place: there is a free car park just around the corner in Station Road.

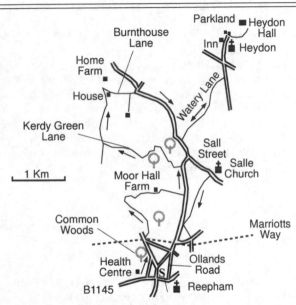

From the Market Place head uphill along the B1145, Dereham Road. Turn right into Smugglers Lane and, at a T-junction, turn left. Go under a railway bridge and immediately turn right over a stile. Follow the hedge on your left through three fields. About 30 yards before the end of the third field (at a wooden cattle pound) bear half-right through a gap in a wire fence. Cross an earth bridge to a signed stile. Cross and turn right across the field, aiming at a grey house in the distance. Cross a stile at the far side and follow the hedge on your left through a gate. Turn left between farm buildings. Pass Moor Hall Farm, **Salle**, on your left and go along the concrete drive to a road. Turn left for 800 yards, then, as the road bends sharp right, turn left up a wide sandy track. This part of the route is not as on the Pathfinder map.

Follow the track past a wood on your right and continue to a T-junction. Turn right along a wide green lane, following it for 1300 yards, until just after a house on your right, where track has become tarmac. Here, turn right along a wide sandy track, following it to a road. Turn right along the road for just under 1 mile. About 150 yards after the road bends left there is a signed bridleway on the left.

The longer route makes a detour to Heydon here, rejoining the shorter route at this point. Turn left along the narrow, enclosed, aptly named Watery Lane, following it for 1 mile to a road. Turn left to a crossroads. Go straight ahead (dead end) into **Heydon**. Take your time to explore this lovely spot: walkers may browse in the parkland beyond the park gates. Retrace your steps back to rejoin the shorter route in the road near Salle.

Continue along the road (turn left if you have taken the longer detour) to reach a fork. Take the left branch (Sall Street) to reach Salle Church. The door is usually open but you will need a torch if you wish to climb the tower. Continue along the road past the church and, at the end of the hedge to the last house on your right, turn right into a field and head for a conifer wood. Keep the wood on your right through two fields and, at its end, cross the field towards the opposite right corner. Go through a gap in the hedge and immediately turn left, away from a road, along an enclosed footpath, following it to a road. Cross and go ahead down Orchard Lane. Go under a railway bridge and immediately turn right up steps to the trackbed (Marriott's Way). Turn left and follow the trackbed to a road. Maintain direction along the road, but where it bends left, turn half-left into Ollands Road. Opposite the church in **Reepham**, turn right uphill to return to the Market Place.

POINTS OF INTEREST:
Salle – Pronounced Sawl and with a variable spelling! The church here (to St Peter and St Paul) was built in the 15th century by six trade guilds connected with the weaving industry - a major source of wealth for the local economy at the time. 'Salle' is derived from Sallow Wood - sallow being the old name for the willow.
Heydon – Heydon Hall is 16th-century and is home to the Bulwer-Long family. The village is frequently used as a film set for period dramas. Look for the horseshoe mare and foal outside the village blacksmith.
Reepham – This too has played its part in several film dramas - the Market Place has had many cameo roles. The town sign in the churchyard was made by pupils at the local high school.

REFRESHMENTS:
There is plenty of choice in Reepham and an inn, *The Earle Arms*, at Heydon.

Walk 70   **WORSTEAD**   7m (11km)

Maps: OS Sheets Landranger 134; Pathfinder 862.
Echoes of Norfolk's past industries.
Start: At 303261, the car park at the rear of Worstead Church.

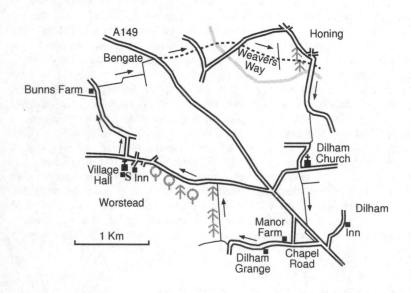

From the car park (between the Village Hall and the New Inn) head north to the main village road. Cross and continue ahead along a minor road. Ignore a road from the right, continuing to a large farm, on your left, where the road bends left. Now turn right over a plank bridge and stile into a field. Continue with a wire fence and ditch on your left and, at the end of the field, cross a stile and turn left. Go through a waymarked gap in a hedge and turn right. Continue with a ditch on your right and, at the end of the field, turn left, as waymarked, at a T-junction of paths. At the next waymarker, turn right and follow the hedge on your right to enter an enclosed green lane. Follow the lane into the hamlet of Bengate. The lane becomes tarmaced: continue along it towards the busy A149. Just after the lane bends sharp right, turn left into an underpass beneath the A149. On the far side, turn right along a disused railway track, joining **Weavers Way**. Go along the top of the embankment and, after 600 yards, cross a minor road to continue along Weavers Way. The Way now crosses a wooden bridge over the old **Dilham Canal**.

Continue through the remains of an old station (there is an information board here) then cross another minor road. Continue along Weavers Way, crossing a farm track, then, just before an iron bridge carries a road over the track, leave the Way by turning left through a wicket gate on to a path leading to a road. Turn right, following the road for $^1/_2$ mile, crossing two bridges, to reach a 'Road Bends' sign. Just before this, turn right along a bridleway, keeping a hedge on your left. At the end of hedge turn right (as waymarked) and continue with a hedge on your left. Follow the hedge as it bends right, then left and, at its end, turn right, as waymarked, to reach a road. Go straight up the road (which is also a bridleway), passing the towerless Dilham Church on your left. Cross a road and continue along the bridleway opposite to reach the main A149. Cross, with care, and go through the wooden barrier opposite. Turn left along a signed path, following a headland. Turn right along Chapel Road (signposted for Sloley), ignoring a road from your right at Manor Farm. Continue past Dilham Grange and, where the road bends sharp left, continue ahead up a concrete drive towards woodland to reach a gate. Turn right along a bridleway, walking with a wood on your left to reach a road. Turn left and follow the road into **Worstead**. Ignore roads to both left and right, continuing to reach the church. Turn left, then fork right into the car park.

POINTS OF INTEREST:
Weavers Way – This is a 56 mile route linking Cromer and Yarmouth. Here it uses a section of track which linked Kings Lynn and Yarmouth until 1959.
Dilham Canal – The canal is now a sorry remnant of a once prosperous waterway linking North Walsham with Yarmouth. Flat-bottomed wherries would have travelled this route.
Worstead – This was an important weaving centre in the late middle ages. Yes – Worsted cloth is named after the town. The church testifies to the wealth of the area then. The wire netting atop the church wall is not to keep spirits in, but rather the Norfolk Horn sheep which graze the churchyard. To make a traditional Norfolk hacking jacket, first catch your sheep…

At the end of July each year, the Worstead Festival is held, a cross between an extended village fete and a country show, with something to suit all tastes and ages.

REFRESHMENTS:
The New Inn, Worstead.

CLAXTON   7m (11km)

Maps: OS Sheets Landranger 134; Pathfinder 903.

A walk with panoramic views of the Yare Valley and an especially good one for church lovers.

Start: At 328032, St Andrew's Church, Claxton.

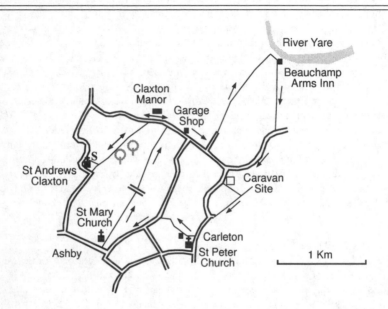

Leave the churchyard at its east corner, following a path through small trees and a hedge. Continue with a fence on your right, passing the rear of some cottages. Go through a hedge to reach a sandy track, turn left and walk downhill to a road. Turn right and follow the road through Claxton. Ignore a road off to the right and, at the end of the council houses, turn left along Mill Lane. At its end, continue ahead along a bridleway, with dykes both left and right, to reach the river. Turn right along the riverbank, following it to the Beauchamp Arms Inn. Now follow the drive to the inn, and the sailing club, to reach a minor road.

Turn right, then take the next road on the left (signposted Carleton/Thurton, Ferry Road). At the end of the caravan site on your left, turn left along a footpath, walking with a hedge on your left and a wire fence on your right. At a T-junction, turn right along a sandy track, following it to a road. Turn left then, after 300 yards, turn right up a sandy drive to a cottage. Dogs on lead here, please, as there are free range hens! Just before the cottage, turn right along an enclosed footpath, following it over a wooden bridge. Continue along the path as it winds between horse paddocks, ignoring all stiles into the paddocks and paths off to the right, to reach a road.

Turn left. Now ignore the road off to the left, continuing to reach a sharp right-hand bend. Here Chapel Road becomes Church Road: just after the first house on your right, turn right into a field along a footpath to the right of a brown gate. Cross the field on a clear path, then maintain direction across a small second field and continue with a hedge on your left, going uphill. The path meets a sandy track at the brow of the hill: follow this track, ignoring farm tracks off to both left and right, to reach a road. Turn left, then left again after 250 yards to go along a sandy bridleway opposite **Claxton Manor**. Follow this track for 800 yards to reach a road. Turn right to return to **St Andrew's Church**.

POINTS OF INTEREST:
St Andrew's Church – The church is 14th-century and epitomises the Norfolk rural church, standing squat and proud, yet without pretensions of grandeur. A statement of quiet dependability. The church has a fine thatched roof, the detail of which is clearly displayed inside.

Claxton Manor – The Manor is built on the ruins of a castle. It is in private ownership - a considerable burden for the present resident. The owner represented Great Britain in the Three Day Event at the Olympics: hence the large equine population. In times past the Yare here was considerably broader and deeper and travellers would have witnessed Roman vessels sailing upstream to supply Venta Icenorum, south of Norwich. They would also have seen raids by Danes - hence the fortifications.

The plume of white smoke seen in the distance on the walk is actually steam from the cooling chimney of the Cantley sugar beet factory. Here beet is processed into sugar and cattle feed. The faint whiff of sweet baked potato issues from the same spot.

REFRESHMENTS:
The Beauchamp Arms Inn, on the walk. The inn has extended opening during the summer.

Maps: OS Sheets Landranger 133; Pathfinder 882.
A pretty village walk: easy paths connecting many churches.
Start: At 054111, All Saints' Church, Mattishall.

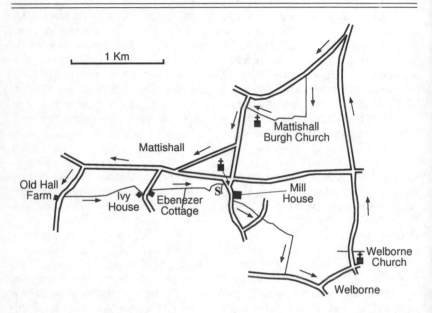

From the church, turn right down Mill Street. At Mill House turn left along a
footpath. Cross a stile (waymarked for the Circular Walk) into a field and follow the
fence on your right to cross a second stile. Cross the field beyond, aiming for the
trees on the opposite side, to reach a minor road. Cross and continue ahead along the
bridleway opposite (also signed for the Circular Walk). Where the track bends left at
a waymarker, turn right into a field. Now keep a pond on your left and go diagonally
leftwards across the field. Walk along the hedge on the left, then go through a gap in
the hedge. Turn right and leave the Circular Walk by following the dyke on the
right. At the field end, turn left for 5 yards, then turn right over a wooden bridge and
follow a path along the left edge of a field to reach a road.

Turn left to Welborne. Take the first road on the left (Church Road) to the church, then turn left into Church Lane. Cross a road and continue ahead along Blind Lane to reach a T-junction. Turn left, uphill, and, after 600 yards, turn left again and follow the hedge on the right across two fields. Maintain direction across a third field (aiming for the telegraph poles) and, at its end, continue along a green lane. At a telegraph pole and waymarker, turn right and follow a path across a field. Follow the hedge on the right as it swings left, then right. The path becomes a green lane: continue along it, passing Mattishall Burgh Church, on your left, to reach a road. Turn left. Ignore the Circular Way when it goes off to the right, continuing for 500 yards to reach a road fork.

Turn right, following the road to a T-junction. Turn right and walk through Mattishall. Just after the de-restriction sign, turn left (signposted Hingham/Garveston - Old Hall Road) and follow the road to Old Hall Farm. There, turn left along a footpath, crossing a field to reach a gap in the hedge opposite. Continue along the path which follows field headlands and then swings right to pass Ivy House, on the right. Go along the drive to a road. Turn left for 100 yards, then, just after Ebenezer Cottage, turn right over a stile to reach an enclosed footpath. At its end, turn left and follow a path, with a hedge on your left (there are waymarkers throughout). The path becomes enclosed and passes behind two schools: follow it to a gravel lane and turn right to return to the start.

POINTS OF INTEREST:
Many of the paths in this area — which are well walked and a credit to the local residents and councils — make up waymarked routes which are part of the Eight Parishes Project — an attempt to celebrate the life of Parson Woodforde, the 18th-century diarist and *bon viveur* who lived locally.

Count the number of churches which you can see along the way — they are evidence of past times when the area was more heavily populated by both humans and the sheep from which they gained a livelihood. Today the area is relatively unspoilt and has kept its character. Mattishall has two schools, inns and thriving shops offering tasty treats for a hungry walker. Try the real butcher and bakery at the start.

REFRESHMENTS:
There is plenty of choice in Mattishall.

Maps: OS Sheets Landranger 133; Pathfinder 883.
Waymarked Parish walk over pleasant farmland.
Start: At 302149, All Saints' Church, Bell Lane, Salhouse.
NB. The church is not in the village.

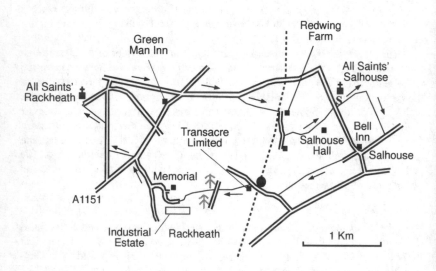

From **All Saints' Church, Salhouse,** turn left down an enclosed green lane. Ignore a footpath to the left, but turn right along another footpath 30 yards further. Now keep a hedge on your right to reach Salhouse's village street. Turn right to a junction by the Bell Inn, going half-right there up Hall Drive (signposted Salhouse Station footpath). At the end of the road go ahead along a track, later passing a farm on your left. The track becomes a gravel drive: follow it to a road.

Turn right, go under a railway bridge and, as the road bends right, 20 yards after Transacre Ltd on your left, turn left through a hedge on to a footpath. Cross a field aiming for a mast in the trees, go through the belt of trees and maintain direction to enter an **Industrial Estate**, passing an old World War II building. Go up a concrete drive to a road (Wendover Road). Turn right and follow the road as it bends left to reach a road (a detour along Bidwell Road, the second turning right leads to the World War II Memorial). Turn right to a T-junction. Cross and turn left, with care, along the busy A1151.

After 50 yards, turn right along a footpath, with a tall hedge on your right. Follow the hedge as it bends right, then left. Go through a gap and maintain direction with the hedge now on your left to reach a road. Turn right and, after 400 yards, turn left along a footpath, crossing two fields aiming towards a church. At **All Saints', Rackheath**, turn right down a tarmac drive to reach a road. Turn left, then left again and, at a T-junction, turn right and walk to the A1151.

Cross, with care, and go along the road opposite (signposted for Salhouse). After 800 yards, where the road bends left, turn right along a footpath across a field. Cross two further fields to reach the railway. Cross, with care, to reach a road at Redwing Farm. Turn right and follow the road as it bends left, then right. At the right bend, turn left along a footpath, following the hedge on your left to a wood. Here, turn left over a stile and continue in your original direction with the wood on your right. Follow a path across a field, with Salhouse Hall on your right, to reach a road. Cross to return to the start.

POINTS OF INTEREST:
All Saints' Church, Salhouse – The church has a reed-thatched roof. This material is still in use – there is a working thatcher in Salhouse village. Reed is durable, lasting up to 60 years. Harvesting is a thankless chore though, as it is a winter job and the reed is cut and stacked with little mechanised help, the harvesters facing bitter winds standing knee deep in icy water!
Rackheath Industrial Estate – This stands on the site of a World War II airfield. From March 1944, B24 Liberator bombers of the USAAF flew 212 missions from this spot. The setting for the Memorial to those who died is perhaps, an apt comment on the futility of War.
All Saints' Church, Rackheath – This church is miles from anywhere! Historians have evidence that the village, in times past, was much closer.

REFRESHMENTS:
The Bell Inn, Salhouse.
The Green Man, is a little off the route on the A1151.

Walk 74   MUNDHAM AND SISLAND   7m (11km)

Maps: OS Sheets Landranger 134; Pathfinder 924.

A walk with panoramic views of farming Norfolk.

Start: At 334978, the Garden House Inn, Mundham.

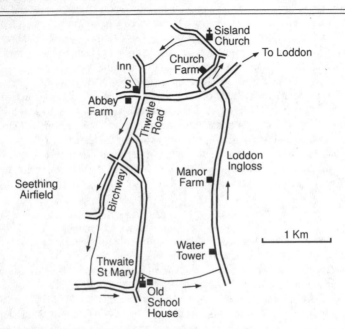

From the inn, cross the road and head south along Thwaite Road to reach a junction. Continue ahead along Birchway to reach a crossroads. Continue straight on along the 'No Through Road' (Birchway), but where the road bends sharp right, continue ahead along a green lane, following it to a road. To the right from here is the airfield at **Seething**.

Turn left to a T-junction and turn left again, soon passing the church at **Thwaite St Mary** on your right. Now, just after a Victorian post box, turn right along gravel drive. Pass the Old School House, on your right, then continue ahead along the gravel footpath. At the top of a rise, where the gravel path swings left, continue ahead along a footpath, walking with a fence on your left.

At the end of a paddock, go through a gap in the hedge on your right and then continue in your original direction, walking with a hedge on your left. Go past a wood on the right, keeping close to the hedge on your left. At the end of the field, maintain direction along a clear path across the next field to reach a minor road.

Turn left, following the road for $1^3/_4$ miles, passing a water tower and then Manor Farm on your left, to reach a T-junction. Turn left, then take the next road on the right (signposted for Sisland), going past Church Farm, on your left, to reach a junction. Turn left, uphill, passing the delightful Sisland Church. Just beyond the church, opposite the Wildflower Centre, turn left along a footpath, crossing a field to pick up a hedge on your left. Maintain direction across the next field, still with the hedge on your left and, at the hedge corner, cross the field aiming between a copse, on the right, and power lines, on the left. Continue westwards, with a hedge now on your right, to reach a road.

Turn left to return to the start in **Mundham**.

POINTS OF INTEREST:

Thwaite St Mary – This is immaculate and has, not surprisingly, won several 'Best Kept Village' awards.

Seething – The name means 'Sitha's people'. The airfield is a remnant of World War II, and is now the weekend haunt of small plane junkies. Views must be spectacular from up high since this area is the Plateau region of Norfolk, a flat, raised table of heavy clay land.

Mundham – Abbey Farm, the large farm opposite the inn at the start of the walk, keeps Simmental cattle - the large white and gold beasts seen in the fields.

REFRESHMENTS:

The Garden House Inn, Mundham, at the start and finish of the walk.

Walk 75   MARTHAM AND WEST SOMERTON   7m (11km)

Maps: OS Sheets Landranger 134; Pathfinder 884.

Visit the Somerton Giant and view his modern counterparts.

Start: At 475196, St Mary's Church, West Somerton.

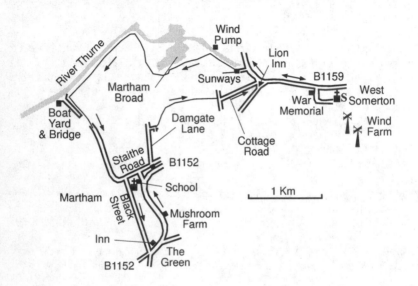

From the church car park, follow the track back to the main road, bending right to reach the War Memorial. Turn left, with care, along B1159, passing the Lion Inn and walking through the village (the road is signposted for Sea Palling/Horsey). Just after the Old Post Office Cottage, on your left, turn left along Staithe Road, following it to Staithe Farm. There, fork left and, just after Sunways, on your right, turn right through a kissing gate and follow the footpath beyond with a dyke on your right.

The path turns slightly inland after passing a windpump on the opposite bank: continue along this clear, waterside path with Martham Broad, and then the River Thurne, on your right. Opposite a boatyard, the path turns inland: you are now walking with a dyke on your right.

Go through a gate to reach a road and continue ahead, going uphill into **Martham** village. At a junction just after the road bends sharp left, turn right along Black Street (signposted for the village) to reach the village green. Turn left, passing the King's Arms on your left. There are shops and a pond here too.

Follow the main road (the B1152) through the village, passing a mushroom farm on your right. Now, just after the school, turn left along School Road to reach a T-junction. Turn right along Staithe Road and, opposite No. 56, turn left along Damgate Lane. Opposite No. 21, turn right into Damgate Back Lane.

At Woodside, fork left along a footpath. Cross a stile to the left of a green barrier and continue along the track beyond. The track bends right: continue with a hedge on your left and, where the hedge ends, continue along a clear path, heading eastwards across a field. Now maintain direction, with a hedge on your left, to reach a road.

Turn right, then left along Cottage Road (signposted for Winterton), following it to the main road. Continue ahead, passing Lion inn, on your right, and retracing the outward route to start by turning right at the War Memorial.

POINTS OF INTEREST:

Martham – This was a Saxon settlement, the name meaning 'The village of the Martens'. The martens are probably polecats – a ferret-like creature found on the marshes here up to 200 years ago. The area was flooded in the 1953 floods. The views are typical Broadland, where the sails of the boats seem to float above ground level and appear magically from behind trees. At the end of the river section of the walk there is a swing bridge for getting tractors across to the marshes opposite.

Robert Hales, the Somerton Giant, is buried in the north-east corner of the churchyard at the start of the walk. He was said to be 7ft 8ins tall. Perhaps fittingly his grave is overlooked by the graceful towers and sails of a modern wind farm. This 'green' energy source is not without its critics for the sails interfere with TV reception! There is also a risk from chunks of ice flying off the blades in cold weather.

REFRESHMENTS:
The Lion Inn, West Somerton.
The New Inn, Martham.
The King's Arms, Martham.

Walk 76   WELLS-NEXT-THE-SEA AND WARHAM   7m (11km)

Maps: OS Sheets Landranger 132; Pathfinder 819.

Tranquil sea marshes which are a riot of colour when the sea lavender is in bloom.

Start: At 917438, the pay and display car park, Wells Quay.

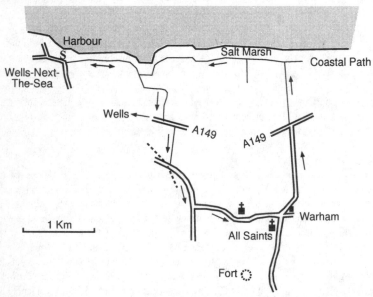

From the car park, head eastwards along the quay to where the road turns right, uphill. There, go straight on, with the Chandlery on your right. Go past the Sailing Club, also on your right, to reach a fork. Take the left-hand branch, following a track between whelk sheds and garages. Continue along the track as it rises on to the seawall.

Continue along the seawall. Later, this bends right: go through a gate and, as the bank turns left, keep straight ahead, going down the bank on a clear grass track which turns left, then right, uphill, to reach the main road (the A149).

Turn left, with care, for 200 yards, then turn right along a wide track. Go past a barn, on your left, and continue along the track to reach a road at a light railway bridge.

Turn left along the road for $^1/_2$ mile, then turn left again along a road signposted for Warham. Enter the village and pass Mary Magdalene Church, on your left, and All Saints' Church, on your right – yes, there are two churches in this tiny village.

At the crossroads by the village inn, turn left and walk to the main road (the A149). Cross, again with care, and continue along the track opposite, heading towards the marshes. Go through a gate and turn left along the Coastal Path. Follow this clear path between farmland and marsh for two miles back into Wells, meeting the outward route near the whelk sheds. Now reverse the outward route back to the Quay.

POINTS OF INTEREST:

Wells-Next-The-Sea – This is still a small trading port, though silting of the creek limits vessel size. It is also still a fishing port for crabs, lobster and whelks. However, it is now predominantly the haunt of the small boat owner. A wooden sailing barge still makes a monthly appearance, bringing fertiliser from Europe: it is part-crewed by German young offenders. 'Next-The-Sea' is a slight misnomer for, at low tide, the water is very, very distant. The faint of heart may care to leave their vehicles elsewhere for it is a long drop should you fail to put the hand brake on!

Warham – About $^1/_2$ mile south of the village is an Iron Age hill fort. It is the best preserved of East Anglian forts with the remains of two ramparts and a ditch enclosing a 3 acre site. It is open to the public.

REFRESHMENTS:

There are numerous opportunities in Wells and an inn, *The Three Horseshoes*, at Warham.

Walk 77   **THE GREAT EASTERN PINGO TRAIL**   7m (11km)
Maps: OS Sheets Landranger 144; Pathfinder 922.
A section of Peddars Way and a wilderness walk.
Start: At 941966, the Pingo Trail car park on the A1075 near
Stow Bedon.

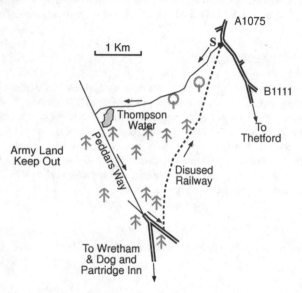

This walk follows a County Council Waymarked Circular Route: follow the green circles with the yellow feet waymarkers.

From the car park, go over the stile to the right of the information board and head north along the track beyond. Follow this clear track through wetland and trees. The track can be wet, but is boardwalked at the worst spots. Go past **Thompson Water**, on your left, to meet **Peddars Way**.

Turn left, south-eastwards, and follow the Way for 2 miles to reach a road fork. Take the left-hand branch, then, after about 500 yards, just before a bridge, turn left along a footpath, crossing grass to reach an **old railway** track. Turn left along this to return to the start.

144

POINTS OF INTEREST:

Thompson Water – Geographers are fans of pingos for they are signs that an area was subject to very cold conditions in the past. With imagination in this area of the walk, you may spot depressions in the soil surrounded by an earth ring about 20 yards across. 10,000 years ago it was a little too chilly to paddle at Cromer as an ice sheet lurked in the Wash. Breckland was a little like modern-day northern Canada and the soil was frozen. In areas where the soil had been waterlogged, the water turned to ice which expanded as it froze and lifted above the surrounding land in a large lens shape. Over the years the top layer of the hump wore off and slid down the sides of the pingo. When the land thawed there was less soil in the centre of each pingo thus leaving the central pit. Where had the missing soil gone? Around the rim – hence the circular rampart.

Peddars Way – This is a waymarked National Trail linking the Icknield Way at Knettishall Heath with the North Norfolk Coastal Path at Hunstanton. There is debate as to its ancient history. The present route was established subsequent to the Iceni revolt led by Boudica in 61AD, but probably usurped one of many ancient routes, possibly dating back to 800BC.

Old Railway – Now part of a County Council path, known as the Great Eastern Pingo Trail, the old railway here was part of the Great Eastern network. This line linked Thetford and Dereham.

REFRESHMENTS.

None en route, but there is an inn and a shop at Great Hockham, a couple of miles to the south, and a mile further south again, on Peddars Way in Wretham, is the *Dog and Partridge Inn*.

145

Maps: OS Sheets Landranger 132; Pathfinder 881.

Peaceful lanes around the Upper Nar Valley. A chance for education too.

Start: At 974169, the Rural Life Museum car park, Gressenhall.

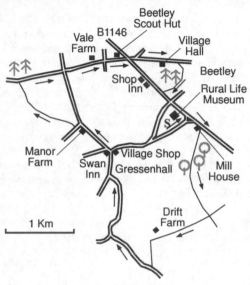

To reach the Museum and car park, follow the brown signs from the B1146, to the north of East Dereham.

From car park, return to B1146 and turn right, with care, towards Dereham. Turn right into a 'No Through Road', with Mill House on your right, and, after the Hermitage, continue ahead along a footpath. Follow the path for just under a mile to reach a junction of paths.

Turn right and walk past Drift Farm, on your right, continuing along its drive, which soon turns sharp left to reach a road. Turn right and, at the next junction, keep right along a road signposted for Gressenhall. At the next junction keep right again, now on a road signposted for Beetley, following this road into the village of Gressenhall.

Go pass the Village Store and Green, on your right, and the Swan Inn, on your left, to reach the main village road. Cross half-left into Bittering Street and continue north-westwards. Go past Manor Farm, on your left, then take the next road on the left. After about 50 yards, turn right along an enclosed footpath, signed as part of the Nar Valley Way. Follow this path to a minor road.

Turn right and, at the next junction, continue ahead, passing Vale Farm on your left. Keep straight on at next junction, passing Beetley Scout Hut, on your left, to reach the B1146. Turn right, with care, and, after 20 yards, turn left along a road signposted for Old Beetley.

Ignore a road off to the left, passing Beetley Village Hall, on your right, and then turning right along a footpath signposted for Fakenham Road. Follow this footpath to reach the B1146 again. Turn left and walk downhill, taking the second turn to the right to return to the **Museum**.

POINTS OF INTEREST:

Gressenhall Rural Life Museum – This is the site of an old workhouse – doesn't it look the part? Today it is a museum devoted to the history of Norfolk agriculture and village life. The site has a working farm complete with heavy horses and makes an ideal family day trip. The estate has some short, waymarked routes along the valley bottom, through the water meadows. Consult Tourist Information etc for Museum opening times and also for the special events such as Harvest Days. The Museum has a thriving Friends Group with many volunteers providing wardens. The Friends make stunning cakes!

REFRESHMENTS:

The Swan Inn, Gressenhall.
There is a teashop at the Rural Life Museum.

Maps: OS Sheets Landranger 132; Pathfinder 860.
Field paths passing a medieval village and a ruined castle.
Start: At 895212, Tittleshall Church.

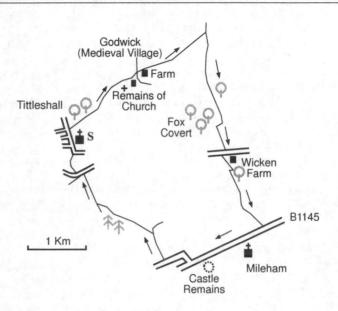

From the church, turn right along the road. Just before the second road on the left, turn right along a signed path, going diagonally across a field, heading just to the right of some trees towards a gap (to the left of two tall trees). At the field edge, go through a gap, over a footbridge and cross the next field towards the hedge, with a ruined church to your right, aiming to the left of two metal gates. Go through the gate and follow the rough track beyond, going between oak trees with a large barn on the right (part of **Godwick** medieval village). Join a track and cross a stile to reach a track in front of farm buildings. Turn right through a gate to the left of buildings and cross a field to a gap by a telegraph pole. Follow a track across the next field to pass between two trees, and continue through a hedge gap to reach a signpost to the left of a second metal pole.

Cross a footbridge over a ditch and bear slightly right across the next field, aiming just to the right of the telegraph poles. Go through the hedge and head towards a bungalow. At the next hedge, go through a gap and turn right along a broad track, with a hedge on your right. Where the hedge turns right at a footpath sign, turn left across the head of a ditch, then go right (heading in the original direction) across a field, aiming to the right corner of a small wood (you are heading almost due south). Pass the wood edge and cross the next field to reach the left corner of another large wood. Cross an earth bridge just to the right of the wood corner to reach a narrow path through the wood, turning right after a few yards. After about 100 yards, turn left along a track. At the wood end, go over a bridge and cross a field to reach a gap in the centre of some buildings. Turn right along a road for 130 yards and, where the road bears left, turn left through a gap and walk with a hedge and pond on your left. At the wood, turn right and, at the corner, turn left to walk with trees on your left. At the wood end, bear slightly right across a field to cross a footbridge and stile. Now follow the left edge of a field towards an isolated house. Join a track and go through a metal gate to the left of the house to reach a road. Turn right into **Mileham**, passing the church and castle ruins on your left.

Turn right along Back Lane, following it around to the left. Now just before the green buildings on the left, turn right along a broad track (Nar Valley Way) and, just before the track bears right, turn left over a footbridge. Bear right along a track to reach the right corner of a wood, crossing two wire fences. At the wood corner, turn left over an earth bridge and then right along a track, heading towards the far corner of another wood. Follow a path around the side of the wood and field edge to join a broad track. Turn right, then, at Cokesford Cottage, turn left along a road. Just before a house on the left, turn right over a footbridge, go through a gap and follow the track beyond to a farm. Go through the gate to the left of the farm and along the right edge of the field beyond. At the field end, turn right through a gate and follow the left edge of the next field to a road. Turn left to return to the start.

POINTS OF INTEREST:

Godwick – This is the site of a medieval village with a ruined church and manor house. The great barn, now partly restored, is just to the right of the path.

Mileham – In addition to the fine church the village has the remains of a castle and a medieval deer park.

REFRESHMENTS:

Only a village shop at Mileham. There is an inn at Litcham, about 2 miles to the south of the start.

Walk 80   REEPHAM   7¹/₂m (12km)

Maps: OS Sheets Landranger 133; Pathfinder 861.
An historic tour of churches in rural Norfolk.
Start: At 100228, Reepham Market Place.

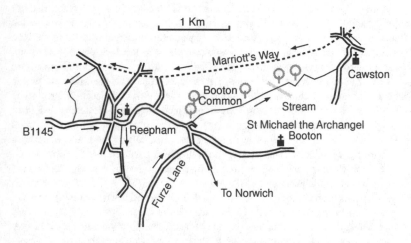

From the Market Place head downhill along Norwich Road, then turn right into Church Street and follow it as it swings right and becomes Back Street. Turn left into Bar Lane just before the Greyhound Inn and follow it to its end. Continue ahead along Whitwell Street and go straight on at a 'Dead End' sign. The road bends right after Anglebury, on your left: turn left over signed stile and follow the path beyond across a field to a wooden bridge.

Cross and walk with a fence on your right to reach a road (Furze Lane). Turn left for ³/₄ mile to reach the main Norwich road. Turn left, downhill. Now ignore the first road off to the right, then turn right into The Street (unsuitable for cars). After 40 yards the road bends right: go straight on up a green track, passing a Norfolk Naturalist Trust sign to enter the woods on **Booton Common**.

Follow a clear path through the woods, a clearing and woods again, keeping a hedge and field to your right. After ¹/₂ mile, the path swings sharp left (look for the Norfolk Naturalist Trust waymarker). Here, continue ahead, leaving the wood and entering a field. Cross the field aiming to the right of the wood in the distance. If the field is ploughed or difficult, then keep to the left edge, following this to the wood. Walk with the wood on your left, and, at its far end, turn left and cross a stream in a ditch. Walk uphill towards the left edge of the copse on the skyline. Join a farm track at the edge of the copse and follow it to a minor road. Note - this track is not as shown on the Pathfinder map; a footpath cuts the corner of the track, but the path is not marked on the ground and the landowner prefers the track to be used.

At the road, turn left into **Cawston**. At the T-junction turn left (or right for the village inn and shop). At a bridge, turn left over a stile and go down steps to a railway path. Follow this to its end at Reepham Moor, heading south-westwards. Continue ahead through a gate and cross a road where it bends left. Rejoin the railway path under a railway bridge and, about 700 yards after rejoining, where the railway crosses a road, turn right down steps on to a road. Turn right under the railway to reach a road fork. Take the right-hand branch and, after 50 yards, turn right along a green track (**Marriott's Way**). Follow the track to the main road and turn left (with care, this road is busy and narrow), uphill, to return to **Reepham** Market Place.

POINTS OF INTEREST:

Booton Common – As you leave the Common look right. The double pinnacles belong to the rather grand St Michael the Archangel Church, Booton. This amazing Victorian church was built by the rector Whitwell Elwin. It remained in use for only 80 years and is now maintained by the Churches Conservation Trust. It is usually open to the public.

Cawston – Inside St Agnes' Church is a balcony built with money raised by sales of church ale. Slightly less holy ale is available from the brewery in Reepham.

Marriott's Way – This is a byway along the remnants of the Midland and Great Northern railway, Marriott being one of the chief engineers. The M&GN was affectionately known as the 'Muddle and Go Nowhere'.

Reepham – Three churches shared the churchyard at Reepham as the parishes of Reepham, Whitwell and Hackford meet at this corner. Only St Michael's and St Mary's remain today.

REFRESHMENTS:

The Greyhound, Reepham.

There are also other opportunities in Reepham and in Cawston.

Walk 81   STRUMPSHAW AND LINGWOOD   7¹/₂m (12km)

Maps: OS Sheets Landranger 134; Pathfinder 903.

Panoramic views of the Yare valley with a chance to visit a steam museum or an RSPB reserve.

Start: At 355080, the Huntsman Inn, Strumpshaw.

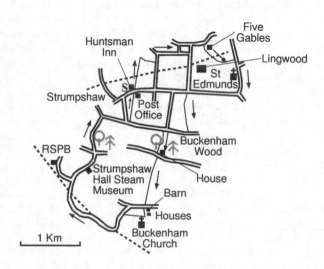

From the inn – which lies opposite the Post Office – follow a footpath northwards, with the inn on your left. Cross the railway, with care, and continue along a gravel track, maintaining direction and walking with a hedge on your left. The track bends right towards some houses and then goes between them: follow a drive to a minor road and turn left. Take the second road to right (Post Office Road) and follow it to a T-junction. Turn left along a road signposted for Acle and Beighton, and follow it to another T-junction. Turn right and then, where the road bends left, turn right again along the drive (which is a footpath) to Five Gables. As the drive bends left, go straight on, over a stile into a field. Cross the field on a clear path going leftwards, then re-cross the railway, again with care. Now follow the clear path across the next field, go through a gap in a hedge and continue with a hedge, and then a fence, on your left to reach a road. Turn right, go past **St Edmund's Church**, on your right, and continue to a T-junction. Turn right towards Norwich.

Follow the road for 1000 yards then, opposite Station Road, turn left along a footpath between houses. Cross a field southwards to reach a minor road. Turn right, then, about 20 yards after passing a road to the right, turn left along a path towards woodland. Follow the clear path to the right, then through the woodland to reach a road.

Turn left, but after 20 yards, turn right along a bridleway, heading downhill across a large field towards Buckenham Church. Cross a minor road and continue ahead, passing a large barn, and then two houses, on your left. Turn right along a footpath to the church, passing it on your left and continuing westwards across a field to a road.

Turn left, downhill, cross the railway, and continue along an 'ex' road. Follow the road to re-cross the railway and continue uphill. Take the first road to the left to reach the **RSPB Reserve**, otherwise keep straight on, passing the **Strumpshaw Steam Museum** on your right. Cross a road and continue, going uphill and passing a wood on your right. Now take the first road to the right, leaving the village. Ignore a road to the left, then, after a further 50 yards, turn left along a footpath, walking with a hedge on your right. Follow this path back to Strumpshaw and the start.

POINTS OF INTEREST:

St Edmund's Church – The church is 12th-century. Buckenham Church, passed later in the walk, is one of only three in Norfolk with an octagonal tower.

Strumpshaw Fen Nature Reserve – The RSPB's Reserve is a 700 acre wetland area. It is home to bitterns and has a wild flower walk.

Strumpshaw Steam Museum – The museum is housed in Strumpshaw Hall and is home to a fine collection of agricultural, fairground and working steam engines. On selected weekends, special events take place which may lead to heavy traffic in the area.

REFRESHMENTS:

The Huntsman Inn, Strumpshaw.

CROSTWICK AND FRETTENHAM 7¹/₂m (12km)

Maps: OS Sheets Landranger 134; Pathfinder 883.

Easy tracks and byways. A walk for horse lovers.

Start: At 257156, a layby on the B1150, on the Norwich side of Crostwick Church.

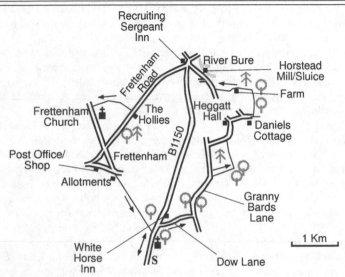

From the layby, turn right, downhill, and walk past the church. Take the second turn right (Dow Lane) and follow it to a T-junction. Turn left (Granny Bards Lane), uphill, and, at the top of the hill, where the road bends left just after red/white/black posts, turn right up a track. After 600 yards, where there is a 'No Entry' sign ahead, turn left along a path, with a hedge on your right, and go past a copse on your left. Continue along the path, still with a hedge on your right, to reach a road.

Turn right, then take the second turn right (Heggatt Street). **Heggatt Hall** is to the left. Go past houses on your left to reach a junction. Fork right and go past cottages on your right. Just after Daniels Cottage, turn left, uphill, along an enclosed track. Walk with a wood on your right and, at the end of the wood, turn left and keep a copse on your right as you head towards a house to join a gravel drive. Continue westwards along the drive, passing a barn on your left. The drive bends left and then right: continue along it to reach a road.

Turn right (Mill Road). Now ignore a minor road off to the left, continuing steeply downhill and passing the sluice and the remains of Horstead Mill on your right before reaching the main road (the B1150) opposite the Recruiting Sergeant Inn. Turn left, then cross the road, with care, and take the first right turn (Frettenham Road). Follow the road uphill for 1 mile, passing The Hollies on your left. At the start of a wood on your left, turn right along a farm track. After 200 yards, fork left into a field and continue along a clear path, with a hedge on your left.

Keep the hedge on your left and continue to reach a drive by Frettenham Church. Go past a house on your left and along drive to a road. Turn left to reach a crossroads in Frettenham. Go straight on along School Road (which is signposted 'Horse') to reach a T-junction. Turn left (Well Green) and, opposite No. 6, turn right along a footpath, with an allotment on your right. Cross a stile on to an enclosed footpath and follow it through a **Horse Sanctuary**. At the end of this, keep straight on, heading downhill with a hedge on your left. At the end of the hedge, maintain direction towards an oak tree.

Now cross wooden and concrete footbridges, then follow a clear, waymarked path through trees and scrub. Bear right along a farm track, cross two drives and continue to reach the main road (the B1150 again). Turn right to return to start.

POINTS OF INTEREST:
Heggatt Hall   The Hall is owned by members of the Gurney family. The Gurneys were a Quaker family with banking interests. Their Norwich bank became part of Barclays in 1896.
Redwings Horse Sanctuary – The Sanctuary is home to at least 300 unwanted or neglected horses, ponies and donkeys. The farm is open to the public on certain days - usually Sundays in summer. Please do not feed the animals along the footpath for your titbits may damage their health or encourage 'bad habits' such as 'asking' all walkers for a snack.

This part of Norfolk is very 'horsey' with many small liveries. Gardeners may appreciate the free horse muck often on offer in Frettenham.

REFRESHMENTS:
The Recruiting Sergeant Inn, Horstead.
The White Horse Inn, Crostwick, just off the route – go along the B1150 beyond Dow Lane.
There are good wild raspberries on the route just after Daniels Cottage.

Walk 83   HETHERSETT $7\frac{1}{2}$m (12km)

Maps: OS Sheets Landranger 144; Pathfinder 902.
Quiet byways around an historic spot.
Start: At 157049, the library, Queens Road Hethersett.

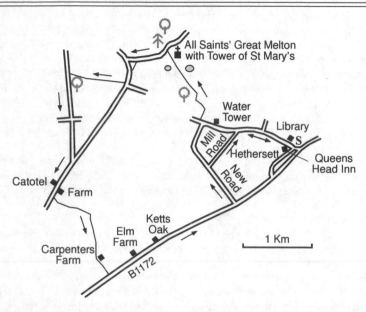

Follow Queens Road away from the old A11 through the village. Go past shops and ignore all side turnings, then, about 200 yards after the water tower and opposite a minor road to Wymondham, turn right along a clear footpath with a hedge and 'doggy bin' on your right.

Follow the hedge as it swings left and, after 200 yards, go through a gap in the hedge and continue along a clear path in the same direction, but with the hedge now on your left. The path swings right, then left, around wood on your left: stay with the path as it heads away from the trees towards power lines. Just before reaching the power lines, turn left along a good track, with a lake on your right, following the track to a road. (All Saints' Church and the 'spare' tower – once of St Mary's Church – are to your right here.)

Turn left, then, just before a memorial at a T-junction, cross the field on the left to reach a road. Turn left and, about 10 yards before a road goes off to the left, turn right along an enclosed (and overgrown!) footpath, following it to a road.

Turn left again and follow the road to a crossroads. Go straight on to reach a T-junction. Turn left, passing a Catotel, on your right, and then a farm, on your left. After a further 50 yards, turn left along a signed farm track, following it, and then a hedge on the right. The track later bends sharp right: continue southwards along it, passing Carpenters Farm, on your left. The track now becomes concrete: continue along it to reach a road (the B1172).

Turn left, using the pavement and taking care as the road can be busy. Go past Elm Farm, on the left, and then **Ketts Oak**, also on the left, in a layby. The tree is enclosed and 'supported'. Continue back into Hethersett and take the first turn left (New Road). After 600 yards, just after the newsagents, turn right along Mill Road. At its end, turn right to pass shops and return to the start.

POINTS OF INTEREST:

Ketts Oak – Under this tree in July 1549 a band of smallholders led by Robert Kett and his brother William met to demonstrate against the injustices of the Enclosures Act which was leading to the fencing of common grazing lands vital to poorer animal keepers. The group marched to Norwich and a band of 20,000 yeoman farmers were eventually defeated in a bloody battle in the Dussindale area of the city. Robert was hanged from Norwich Castle for his treason. His brother from the tower of Wymondham Abbey. The tree still produces acorns. In 1953 a sapling was planted to commemorate the Queen's Coronation. Sadly, this has vanished. In 1993 pupils from Hethersett Middle School planted replacements which are being nurtured. Perhaps the original tree has greater chance of continuing good health now that the A11 has been moved and it is no longer subjected to traffic fumes and vibrations. The tree is also commemorated on Hethersett village sign.

REFRESHMENTS:
The Queens Head, Hethersett, near the start of the walk.
There are plenty of alternatives in Hethersett.

Walk 84   BALE AND HINDRINGHAM   7¹/₂m (12km)

Maps: OS Sheets Landranger 132 and 133; Pathfinder 840 and 841.

A walk offering panoramic views of north Norfolk.

Start: At 011367, All Saints' Church, Bale.

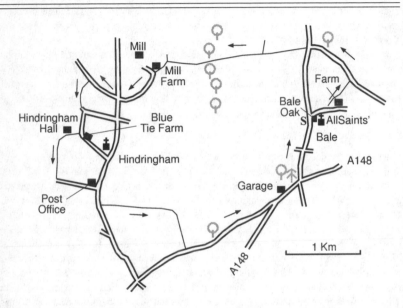

From the church, which stands beside the **village green**, take the road running eastwards, signposted for Sharrington. Pass the Village Hall, and then a farm, on your left and, after a further 100 yards, turn left along a gravel drive. Follow the drive as it bends right, left and right again to reach a road.

Turn left to reach a T-junction. Cross the road and continue straight ahead along the green lane/bridleway opposite. Ignore track off to the right after ¹/₂ mile, continuing to the end of the lane, and then maintaining direction along a clear path towards woodland. At the wood, turn left along a path, then, after 100 yards, turn right over a bridge into the wood. Follow a clear path through the wood and, at the far side, continue in the same direction, walking with a ditch on your left towards a 'headless' mill.

158

When the path reaches a track at the white gates, turn left and follow the track, bending right to reach a road at Mill Farm. Turn left and follow the road to a junction by a telephone box. Turn right, then take the first left turn, signposted for **Walsingham**.

After $^1/_3$ mile, at the top of a rise, turn left along a gravel track (signed as a bridleway). At the end of the track continue southwards along a road, passing large farm buildings on your left. Now turn right along the footpath that follows the drive to **Hindringham Hall**. Go past the hall, on your right, then head southwards along the drive to reach a road.

Turn left to reach a T-junction by the Post Office. Turn right and, after 400 yards, turn left along a gravel bridleway, following it as it bends sharp right to reach a road. Turn left and follow this minor road for 1 mile to reach the **main A148**. Turn left, with care, passing a petrol station/shop and then taking the first road on the left, signposted for Bale, to return to the start.

POINTS OF INTEREST:

Village Green – The Green was once home to the Bale Oak, a mighty oak tree. It was said to be so big that a dozen people could stand inside its hollow trunk. Some also say that a cobbler had his shop inside the oak. Alas, the old tree has long since vanished but the spot – now looked after by the National Trust – is marked by a copse of evergreen oaks.

Walsingham – In 1061 the Virgin Mary appeared at Little Walsingham. The spot has been a shrine ever since.

Also close to the route are the villages of Great and Little Snoring. The name is derived from *Snears People* and is not necessarily a slur on the population!

Hindringham Hall – This part of Norfolk is dominated by flint faced houses. There are good examples all along the route, but one of the best is Hindringham Hall.

Main A148 – Thursford Museum, signed from the main road, is devoted to steam engines in their various guises. It is family run and is renowned for its spectacular Christmas carol concerts – worth a visit but book a year in advance!

REFRESHMENTS:

The shop at the BP petrol station on the A148 is the only possibility on the route, but there are opportunities at Thursford, Walsingham and Fakenham.

Walk 85   **HARPLEY DAMS**   7¹/₂m (12km)

Maps: OS Sheets Landranger 132; Pathfinder 859.

Historic tracks, woodland and rolling farmland.

Start: At 771255, the parking area at Harpley Dams, on the A148.

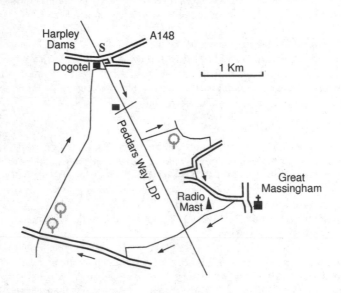

To find the start, turn off the A148 midway between Hillington and West Rudham at the Paradise Dogotel, Harpley following the sign for Great Massingham. Now turn right immediately and then go left along the track beside the wall of the Dogotel (signposted for Peddars Way). The parking area is outside the waterworks on the left.

From the parking area, turn left along **Peddars Way**, heading away from the road. After ³/₄ mile, at the start of the wood on the left, turn left along a track with the wood on your right. Go past a sunken, wooded area on your left and then bear right at a track junction. Follow the track around to the right, then take the right fork at a farmyard, passing between the farmyard and the house to reach a road.

Turn right and, just after a double bend, turn left along a signed, narrow path between hedges to reach a road. Turn left for $1/4$ mile, passing a farm, to reach a row of bungalows on the left. Continue straight ahead for $1/3$ mile to visit **Great Massingham**, returning by same route.

On your return, bear left at the bungalows, following a metalled road (with a footpath sign). Go past radio masts on your right and, where the road turns right, go straight ahead along a stony track to meet a crossing (equally stony) track at a sign for Peddars Way. Continue ahead along a grassy track, with a fence and hedge on the left. Where the visible track ends at a hedge, maintain direction across a field, aiming for the far left corner of a wood (you <u>are</u> on a public footpath). Cross the corner of the wood by a footpath sign, following the right edge of the field. Now, where the trees end, bear slightly right for 5 yards, then turn left to walk with a hedge on your left. At the bottom of a dip, turn left at a footpath sign and walk along the field edge to reach a road.

Turn right and follow the road for about a mile, passing a road and a track on the right, to reach a crossing track. Turn right along this track, following it through a wood and continuing uphill. On reaching a crossing track, with a wood on your left, bear slightly left, then right to continue in the same direction, with trees on your right. Follow the track downhill for nearly a mile, passing through trees to reach a crossing wire fence. Turn right past the Dogotel to reach a crossing track (Peddars Way) and turn right to return to the start.

POINTS OF INTEREST:

Great Massingham – With its brick and flint cottages grouped round the village pond, this is one of the most attractive villages in west Norfolk.

Peddars Way – This National Trail follows a Roman road, part of which may be an even older track, from Knettishall Heath near Thetford to Holme-next-the-Sea near Hunstanton.

REFRESHMENTS:

There is an inn, *The Rose and Crown*, at Great Massingham.

Walk 86   BLICKLING HALL AND BURE VALLEY   8m (13km)

Maps: OS Sheets Landranger 133, Pathfinder 861.

Historic National Trust park, woodland and rolling farmland.

Start: At 176286, the car park at Blickling Hall.

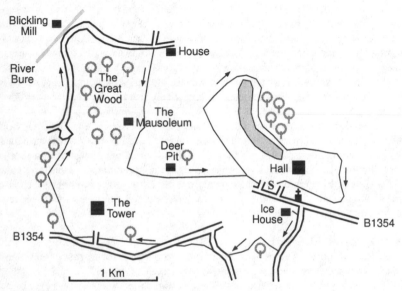

Note: This walk utilises Permissive Paths on National Trust land in part. Please respect the Trust's ground rules, ie. dogs must be on leads.

From the car park, go through the visitor centre (there is no need to pay) to reach the B1354. Turn left, with care, then turn first right towards Silvergate. Walk along the road for 400 yards then turn right over a stile on to an enclosed footpath: there is a blue arrow on a post. Cross two further stiles as you follow the path through a copse and out into an enclosed footpath along the right edge of a field. Go over a cow crossing (which can be soggy if the weather is wet!) into a drive and, after 100 yards, where the drive turns right, uphill, bear left along a green track (blue arrow on post). Go past some cottages, following the track as it swings right to reach the main road again. Cross, with care, and continue along the wide gravel drive opposite.

After 50 yards turn left (blue arrow) on to a forest ride. Follow this across a gravel track leading to a tower on your right. The tower was a viewing platform for a Racecourse on the Estate in the 18th century, but is now a private dwelling.

Continue along the grass track (still following blue arrows) with a copse on your left. At the end of the copse, turn right through a small gate on to a track along the edge of a wood. Follow the track into a car park, exiting to road. Turn right: you are now on the Weavers Way, a long distance path from Cromer to Great Yarmouth. Follow the road, passing Blickling Mill on the river Bure – you may see Angora goats opposite – and 200 yards after passing a barn and gate on your right, turn right along a narrow footpath between two rows of young trees. Follow the path uphill through a gate and into a wood. This is the original estate's Great Wood: follow the wide track eventually leaving the wood, and continuing with trees to your right. After 300 yards, The Mausoleum, a black pyramid, comes into view on your right. At a T-junction, where there is a woodland information board, turn left towards Blickling Hall. You are now back on Weavers Way.

At the next T-junction, the faint of foot can turn right, going through the hamlet of Blickling to reach the car park. The sturdy can continue by turning left along a gravel track, the original route of the Weavers Way. Pass gates and stiles in a belt of trees and immediately turn right along a well-marked grass track with trees on your right. Follow this track to the lake. There, turn left and follow the lake's edge to reach a gate. Go through towards the Hall. As the path meets the Hall garden it swings left: you are on the plebeian side of the Ha Ha - designed to keep deer, sheep and yokels from the gardens without impeding the view. Continue along the well-walked path skirting two sides of **Blickling Hall** gardens, then turn right through a small gate into a copse and continue to a coach car park. Here, turn right for refreshments in the Hall teashop. Those with clean boots may also wish to view the Hall with its display of estate history. To return to the start, turn left from the coach park to reach the main road and turn right back to the car park.

POINTS OF INTEREST:
Blickling Hall – Blickling is derived from the old English *Bekeling* - a meadow around a stream. The estate was once owned by Sir Thomas Boleyn, father of Anne. It is said that Sir Thomas died a broken man vowing to remind the world of her fate. On 19 May, his headless ghost may be seen driving a coach and horses in the area.

REFRESHMENTS:
The Buckingham Arms, Blickling.
Blickling Hall tearooms.

Walk 87　　　　　　　HONINGHAM　　　　　　8m (13km)

Maps: OS Sheets Landranger 133 and 144; Pathfinder 882.
Pleasant tracks in a quiet river valley.
Start: At 102118, opposite the Buck Inn, Honingham.

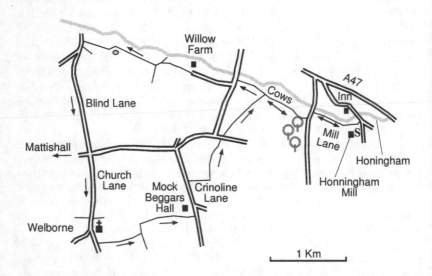

From the village green, go downhill along The Street passing the village pump on your left – don't drink the water! Turn right into Mill Lane and, at its end, cross a stile into a field. Follow a path across rough scrub, crossing a wooden bridge into a copse and continuing to a road. Turn left, then, after 50 yards, turn right over a stile into a field. Keep a wood and fence on your left to reach an ornamental gate into the wood. Turn right, downhill, along a path, go through a farm gate and cross an earth bridge. Turn half-right and cross a field – aiming to the right of three large oaks – to reach a gate. Go through and follow the hedge on your left to reach a gate at the end of the field. Go through and turn right after 10 yards, as **waymarked**, into a copse. Leave the copse through a gate and walk with a hedge on your right, passing the East Tuddenham Charity land and a copse to reach a road.

Turn left and, after 50 yards, turn right to follow a dead end road to Willow Farm. Walk ahead, passing a new barn and then a copse on your left, then crossing a bridge. Now ignore paths off to both left and right, walking ahead into the next field. Keep the hedge on your left until just before a large pond and then head downhill towards the River Tud, following it on a path which crosses several waymarked stiles. Eventually you cross a stile on to a road. Turn left to reach a road junction.

Take the left fork (Blind Lane), following the road for a mile to reach a crossroads. Continue ahead along Church Lane for $^3/_4$ mile to **Welborne Church**. At the road junction, turn right (signed Brandon Parva/Barnham Broom) and, about 200 yards beyond the church, turn left along a bridleway (the track at the end of the hedge). Ignore a farm track off to the right after 10 yards, continuing with a hedge on your left. After $^1/_2$ mile, at a T-junction of tracks, turn left, following a track as it swings sharp right and ends at a farm drive. Turn left to a road. Walk ahead along the road for 300 yards, then turn right along a bridleway (Crinoline Lane), just after Crinoline House.

Keep a hedge on your right and, at its end, turn left, as waymarked and follow a hedge to a stile. Cross and turn left along the left edge of a large field, heading towards East Tuddenham Church. Follow the path through a copse to a road. Cross the road and turn right, then turn left along a path, heading diagonally right across a field, walking downhill towards some trees with a ditch on your right. About 50 yards before the trees the path crosses an earth bridge over a dyke: continue to a gate. Now retrace the outward route to return to the start.

POINTS OF INTEREST:
Waymarking – The paths on this walk are both well marked and well used. They are part of the 'Eight Parishes Project', a joint effort by Parish and County Councils to commemorate an area made famous by the 18th-century diarist Parson Woodforde.
Welborne Church – The church has a round tower as do many in Norfolk. The style is said to be due to the difficulty in making corners with round flints.

REFRESHMENTS:
The Buck Inn, Honingham.

Walk 88   HOLT AND SHERINGHAM   8m (13km)

Maps: OS Sheets Landranger 133; Pathfinder 820.

A splendid coastal walk with a return by steam train.

Start: At 157432, the Station Approach car park, Sheringham.

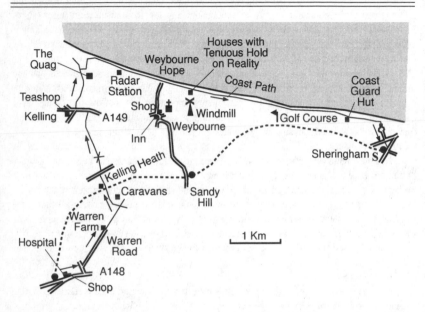

From the car park enter the **North Norfolk Steam Railway** (<u>not</u> the British Rail Station opposite), buy a single ticket to Holt and enjoy a gracious, but slow, uphill journey through **Weybourne** to your destination.

Leave the train at Holt. (Turn right if you wish to visit the town: it is 1 mile, but you can take the Holt Flier, a horse-drawn bus). The walk turns left. At a right bend, continue straight on along the old road, with Kelling Hospital on your left. Continue along the main A148 towards Cromer, with great care, then take the first road on the left, signposted for Kelling. After 150 yards, turn right on Warren Road. Go past Warren Farm and continue straight on along a track on the right edge of a field, following it into Kelling Heath and a caravan site. About 20 yards further on, turn left at a waymarker post and follow a path across a heath to reach a level crossing.

Cross the railway, with care, and continue ahead. Cross a road and maintain direction along a path. After 300 yards, in a clearing, take a very narrow path through gorse: the path you want is just left of straight on and goes downhill. The path becomes a green lane: continue along it to reach the A149. Cross, with care, and turn left. The farmer usually leaves a wide headland in field. This is not a right of way, but many use it for safety. After 250 yards, just before some cottages (there is a teashop on the corner), turn right down a track. After $^3/_4$ mile, turn right along a grass track, following it as it bends left to reach a **shingle bank**. Go up the bank and turn right along the Coastal Path.

Continue along the Coastal Path into Sheringham. Just after the boating pond, turn right to reach a roundabout. Go ahead along The Boulevard, cross Church Street and go up St Peters Road opposite. At its end, turn left to regain the start.

POINTS OF INTEREST:

North Norfolk Steam Railway – The railway is staffed by volunteers. Check the schedule before starting out: you may be lucky to arrive for a special event such as 'Thomas the Tank Engine Day'. The railway charges for carrying dogs.

Weybourne – The remains of a 12th-century Priory can be found adjacent to the church. This part of the coast has always been recognised as a likely invasion spot – hence the 1588 Spanish Armada saying '*He who would old England win must at Weybourne Hope begin*' and the remnants of the World War II defences.

Shingle Bank – The coast here is rapidly eroding. Technically you are walking over 'poorly consolidated boulder clay' which, in layman's terms, is the sand and debris left behind by the last ice sheets to cover East Anglia. Much of this section is 'Rolling Path' – as a chunk falls into the sea the council claim a little more from the adjacent fields.

REFRESHMENTS:

The Ship Inn, Weybourne.

There is plenty of choice in both Sheringham and Holt and, as noted, a teashop in Kelling. In season there is often an ice-cream van at Weybourne beach car park.

Maps: OS Sheets Landranger 134; Pathfinder 924.
Hidden architectural delights around a pleasant market town.
Start: At 362987, the car park adjacent to Holy Trinity Church,
Church Plain, Loddon.

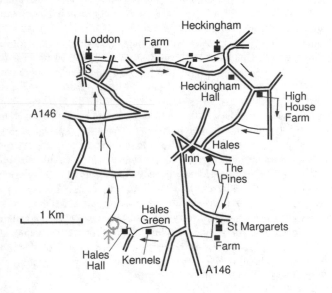

From the car park, go in to the churchyard, leaving along an enclosed footpath in the
north-east corner, as signed by a yellow Broads Authority waymarker. Follow the
path to a road and turn right to reach a T-junction. Turn left along a road signposted
for Norton. Go straight over at a crossroads, following a road signposted for Reedham
Ferry. Go past a farm on your left, then, after 150 yards, at the sign for Riverside
Farm, turn left along a footpath that goes diagonally right across a field. If the field
is divided by wires, crossing points will be indicated by plastic pipe covers. At the
far side of the field, cross stile on to a drive. Turn left, then, after 20 yards, turn right
along a footpath between houses. Cross a stile into a field and cross the field beyond
to another stile. Cross and continue eastwards through rough (!) scrub to a church.
Turn right up a track to a road. Turn right, then fork left into Briar Lane. Go past

Heckingham Hall, then take the first turn left. Go past High House Farm, on the left, to reach a T-junction. Turn right and, after 700 yards, turn right again along a footpath, following the hedge on your left to a road. Turn left into Hales. At the T-junction, turn left and, after 200 yards, just after The Pines, turn right along a footpath between houses. Cross the field ahead and go through the hedge. Turn left and follow the hedge on your left as it bends right, left and right again. At the second right you lose the hedge and follow a headland southwards. Go through a hedge gap and turn right. After about 50 yards (there is a waymarker post hidden in the hedge) turn left along a clear path to a road near **St Margaret's Church**. Cross the road and enter the churchyard, leaving along a path heading southwards through a thicket.

Cross a stile into a field and maintain direction to reach a track. Turn right to the main road (the A146). Cross, with care and turn right, but, soon, take the first turn left, signposted for Hales Hall. Take the first turn right, following a road that becomes 'Privately Maintained' and crosses Hales Green. Go past kennels, on your left, and, after a further 150 yards, turn right along a drive/bridleway to **Hales Hall**. There, just before a wall, turn right along a footpath. Turn left at the end of the wall and, at the end of the buildings, keep straight on along a bridleway to reach a T-junction of tracks. Turn right and follow a clear path to a minor road. Turn left, then, after 20 yards, turn right along a footpath, following a wire fence. Follow the path across a field on the valley floor to reach a stile on to the A146. Cross, with care, and turn left. After 20 yards, just before some rails, turn right along a footpath. Follow the path back into **Loddon**, keeping a stream on your left to reach a road. Turn left and follow the road as it bends right, uphill, to return to the start.

POINTS OF INTEREST:

St Margaret's, Hales – The church has a Saxon round tower and is now in the tender hands of The Redundant Churches Fund.

Hales Hall – What you see is only part of a manor house built by Sir Henry Hobart a servant of Henry VII. The Hall is alongside Hales Green. Greens are areas of common grazing land with small farmsteads set around their perimeters. They were once common in south Norfolk and north Suffolk.

Loddon – This is a prosperous market town and a popular haunt for sailors. The town was once a port. There are many good Victorian and Georgian houses around the town centre. The church is 15th-century, though a church has stood on this spot since the time of Felix, the first Bishop of Dunwich in 631.

REFRESHMENTS:

There is a good choice in Loddon and an inn just off the route in Hales.

Maps: OS Sheets Landranger 134; Pathfinder 923 and 924.
A tour of Greens and Commons.
Start: At 197926, the car park in Swan Lane, Long Stratton.

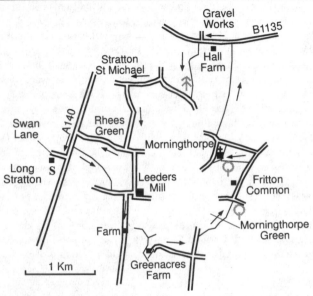

From the car park — which is signed from the A140 — return to main road and turn left, with care, towards Norwich. Now, just before Barclays Bank, turn right into Star Lane and follow it to its end. There continue ahead along a footpath, following it as it bends southwards to reach a road.

Turn left and, just before Leeders Mill, turn right along a road signposted for Wood Green. Go past a farm on your right, then turn left along a gravel track around Wood Green. Ignore a footpath to the left, between houses, and, after passing a pond, continue southwards along a green track to reach Greenacres Farm.

There, ignore the footpath ahead, turning left along a tarmac road. Follow the road to a crossroads and turn left. After 200 yards, bear right over **Morningthorpe Green** and follow a waymarked footpath with a hedge on your right, and young trees on your left. At the end of the hedge, turn right over a plank bridge.

Now continue in your original direction for a further 50 yards, then turn left along an enclosed green lane (Snake Lane). Follow the lane through trees to reach a road at a T-junction (at Fritton Common). Cross and keep ahead along the minor road opposite.

Go past Manor Farm on your left and, after a further 300 yards, turn left into a field. Cross a stile and turn right (look for the red arrow waymarker). Go through a gate and turn left, as waymarked, towards thatched houses. At the end of the long field, go through a gate and immediately turn left over a stile into trees. Follow the path into the churchyard of **St John the Baptist Church**, Morningthorpe. Leave the churchyard on to a road and turn right.

Follow the road to a T-junction, continuing ahead up the gravel track opposite to reach another road (the B1135). Turn left, with care, and follow the road past Hall Farm, on your left, and a gravel pit, on your right. About 50 yards after a 'bend' sign, turn left along a gravel track, following it as it bends right, then left. Now go past a wood on your right to reach a road.

Turn right, then take the first turn left towards Stratton St Michael. Take the next turn left and follow it to a T-junction at Rhees Green. Turn right to return to Long Stratton, turning left, with care, at the main road (the A140) and then right to return to the car park.

POINTS OF INTEREST:

Morningthorpe Green – This area of Norfolk is famous for its Greens. These are open, common grazing areas with farmsteads set around their perimeters. It is, perhaps, the spot in the county where you are most likely to find a retirement 'des res' thatched cottage. A glance at the map shows just how many Greens are to be found here. The map also betrays past history - the main Norwich-Ipswich road is a Roman relic. Further west are farms with strange names such as Cuidad Rodrigo - from the times when Norfolk men fought in foreign parts and returned to their homes with battles and victories to celebrate.

St John the Baptist Church – The church has a 12th-century round tower. Opposite is a 17th-century farmhouse with a timber frame.

REFRESHMENTS:

There is plenty of choice in Long Stratton.

Walk 91   CASTLE ACRE AND WEST ACRE   8m (13km)

Maps: OS Sheets Landranger 132; Pathfinder 880 and 881.

An easy walk through the Nar Valley and over farmland, with good views.

Start: At 816152, the Village Green, Castle Acre.

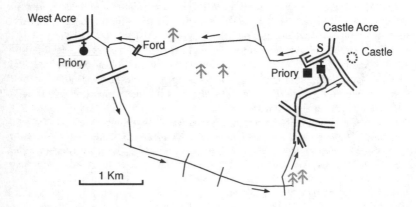

From the village sign, follow the road westwards, with the Ostrich Inn on your right. At the entrance to the **Priory**, follow the road around to the right and, at the next right bend, turn left along a stony track, bearing right after $^1/_2$ mile. Now, just after the river comes close to the road, bear left through a metal gate by a cattle grid and follow the grassy track beyond, with a hedge on your right, and the river on your left. Go under power lines and into woodland. Go through a wooden kissing gate and walk ahead, ignoring a faint track on the left, to reach a cross-tracks in a dip. Go straight ahead, through a metal gate at the wood's end, and continue along a green track. Cross a stile and a wooden bridge, then go over a second bridge with Mill House on your left. Go through a barrier on to a road. Turn right, then, just before a bridge by a ford, turn left along a footpath, ignoring the 'Private' sign. Walk with the river, and then gorse bushes, on your right, ignoring two tracks off to the left to reach a cross-tracks. Go ahead, with a gate on your right, to meet a broad track at some pine trees. Turn right along this track and go over a footbridge to reach the Stag Inn. Turn left along the road to West Acre church and the ruins of the **Priory** behind.

Retrace your steps to the Stag Inn and along the same track to return to the pine trees. Turn right through a gap in the hedge and bear slightly right, then left, walking with a hedge on your right to reach a road. Cross and go straight ahead along a broad track under the power lines. Go past a barn on the left and then go slightly right, uphill. Now, where the track turns right at the end of a field, go ahead for a few yards and then turn left, walking with a hedge on your left – there are good views from here. Shortly you pass a wood with the unusual name of Three-Cocked-Hat Plantation: continue along the track for about $1^1/_2$ miles, crossing two broad tracks to reach a third in a dip with a wood on your left. Turn left here, going uphill with the wood on your right, then bearing right to pass an overgrown pond on your left. Castle Acre church can soon be seen ahead. Pass under power lines to join a road from right, with South Acre church visible to your left. Follow the road to a crossroads (there is a sign here for the Peddars Way/Norfolk Coast Path National Trail). Go ahead, along the road, with good views of Castle Acre Priory on the left. Cross a ford by a footbridge and continue along the road with the river on your right. Where the river bears right, turn right to cross a small footbridge over a ditch and go over a stile. Continue along the path beyond, with the river on your right. Where the river takes a U-bend, continue along the path, eventually rejoining the river. Just before a bridge, the path bears left to reach a stile. Go over on to a road and turn left along it, passing Blind Lane and going uphill. Go past a footpath leading to the **castle**, on your right, then go under an 11th-century archway and turn left to return to the village green.

POINTS OF INTEREST:
Castle Acre Priory – This 11th-century Cluniac Priory stood on land granted to the Earl of Surrey by William the Conqueror.
West Acre Priory – The remains of the Priory include a 14th-century gatehouse. Shakespearean and other plays are performed here in July during the King's Lynn Festival.
Castle Acre Castle – The castle was built by the Normans.

REFRESHMENTS:
The Ostrich, Castle Acre.
The Stag Inn, West Acre.

Walk 92   **BROOKE**   8$\frac{1}{2}$m (13$\frac{1}{2}$km)

Maps: OS Sheets Landranger 134; Pathfinder 924.

Easy tracks and by-ways with a pretty village watering hole.

Start: At 289993, the village pond, The Street, Brooke - opposite the White Lion Inn.

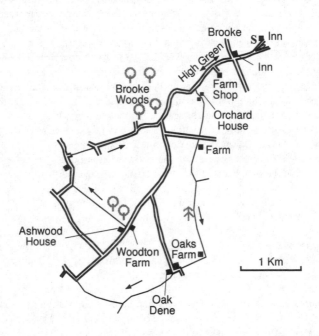

From the pond, turn left towards the centre of the village to reach a junction. Turn right (signposted for Shotesham) and walk to the main road (the B1332). Cross, with care, into High Green. Walk past the farm shop, on the right, then, just after No 69, turn left along a footpath into High Green Gardens. Just beyond Orchard House, on your left, turn left along a fenced footpath. Turn right at the end of the house and continue southwards along an enclosed path. Cross a ditch by means of a plank bridge and continue southwards with a hedge on your left, going through two fields to reach a road.

Cross the road to the bridleway opposite and follow this past a farm, on your left. Now ignore a track off to the left, keeping ahead for 1 mile to reach a T-junction of tracks, with a bungalow on the right. Turn right. The track becomes gravel, then tarmac, and meets a minor road at Oaks Farm.

Continue ahead along the road, then, after 50 yards, keep straight on along a green lane where the road bends sharp right near Oak Dene. Follow this lane for $^3/_4$ mile, then turn sharp right and walk to a road (Fylands Road). Turn right. Ignore a minor road to the left and, just after Ashwood House, turn left along a footpath with a wood, and then a tall hedge, on your right. At the end of the field, keep a market garden patch on your right and maintain your original direction.

Cross a ditch via a sleeper and continue in your original direction with a hedge now on your left, going through two fields to reach a road. Turn right (the **Roadside Nature Reserve** is to your left). Go past a house on your left, then turn right at the gas hydrants to go along a footpath. Follow a headland uphill between fields, then continue with a hedge on your left. Maintain direction across a field to reach a wood and a minor road.

Follow Heath Lane into Brooke, ignoring side roads to rejoin the outward route near the village shop and **Spurgeons Farm Shop**. Now retrace the outward route to return to the start.

POINTS OF INTEREST:
Roadside Nature Reserves – These are managed by the Norfolk Naturalists Trust to encourage a diversity of wildlife and plants. They are not sprayed and mowing is strictly controlled. It obviously pays dividends for the author spotted a weasel and many rabbits in this short walk. It has been calculated that an area the size of Berkshire is available along the road network in Britain – a large Nature Reserve in any country!

Spurgeons Farm Shop – This is a long established family business with their own Jersey cattle (which graze to the south of Brooke) and pigs supplying the shop. A refreshing change in these days of the 'Agribusiness'.

The green lanes used on this walk are 'white roads' on OS maps, but are part of a designated bridle route – the County Council have produced a guide leaflet for horse riders.

REFRESHMENTS:
The White Lion Inn, Brooke.
There are other opportunities in Brooke, or you could bring your sarnies and enjoy the pond. The 'mongrel' ducks here are most persistent - so bring plenty.

Walk 93　　**BLAKENEY AND GLANDFORD**　　8¹⁄₂m (13¹⁄₂km)

Maps: OS Sheets Landranger 133; Pathfinder 820.

Splendid views of a wild and unspoilt coast.

Start: At 028442, the car park, Blakeney Quay.

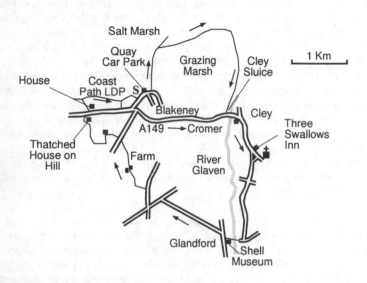

From the car park, follow the footpath northwards along the raised bank opposite the toilets and ice-cream shop (this is part of the Coastal Path National Trail). Ignore a path out into the saltmarsh, walking with a grazing marsh to your right and the saltmarsh/water to your left. One mile further on the path turns right, heading inland: continue along it to reach the A149 at Cley Sluice. Turn left down steps on to the road. Turn left along the road, with great care, but when it bends sharp left at Picnicfare, turn right along a road signposted for Holt. Go past a Post Office on your right and continue to Cley Green: the church and Three Swallows Inn are to your left. Follow the road towards Wiveton, keeping the green on your left, to reach a crossroads. Go straight on, along a road signposted for Glandford and an unbridged ford. Follow the road to a T-junction. Turn right and go over or through the ford. Go past the Shell Museum on your left, cross the main road (the B1156), with care, and head uphill along a minor road to reach a T-junction. Turn left to a crossroads. Turn right, uphill, along a road signposted for Blakeney, then, after 400 yards, turn left through a gate and follow the track beyond. Walk through farm buildings and later, when the track becomes a green lane stay with it, following power lines and descending to reach a road (the B1388).

Cross the road, with care, and go along the drive opposite. Just before a house, turn left and walk with a high wooden fence on your right. Follow the fence as it turns right. At the end of the trees, turn right into a field and immediately turn left to walk with a hedge on your left. At the field corner, turn right and head towards a thatched house on the hill, still walking with a hedge on your left. At the bottom of the house/hill, turn left along a clear path, following it around the hill to reach a gate by a quarry. Go through on to the main road (the A149) and turn right, uphill. Please take care - this is a blind brow and a busy road. At the crest of the hill, turn left along a bridleway. Go past a house on your right, continuing along the path as it descends into the saltmarsh. At a T-junction turn right to follow the Coastal Path into **Blakeney**, ignoring a footpath off to right when you reach the first houses. Continue along a clear path with water on your left to return to the Quay.

POINTS OF INTEREST:

Blakeney – There has been a settlement here since Roman days. In the Doomsday Book it is called *Esnuterlea*. Later this became *Snitterley* – meaning 'a cold wind' or 'to blow – as of the nose'. Try this walk in February and you will see how apt this is. Blakeney was an important port in the 11th-15th centuries, but silting of The Glaven has led to its decline. Coastal defence banks were first constructed in the 17th century. The land formed was initially too salty for agriculture, but the cleansing action of rainwater eventually produced the grazing marshes seen today. The banks are not infallible as the 'High Tide' marks on the Granary bear witness. It is not unknown for cars left on the Quay to receive a good wash!

As silting caused a decline in port trade the community was 'discovered' by the tourist industry. After World War II, the Blakeney Housing Trust was formed to keep some houses for local residents – see the plaques on the walls of several cottages in High Street.

Blakeney Church is unusual in having two towers. No one really knows why there is a 'spare'. Perhaps a beacon for shipping?

REFRESHMENTS:

The walker is spoilt for choice in Blakeney, the opportunities including the best bacon buttie and mug of coffee possible in the small caravan in the Quay car park.

Walk 94   HOLKHAM AND BURNHAM OVERY   9m (14¹/₂km)

Maps: OS Sheets Landranger 132; Pathfinder 819.

Stately parkland with a wild and lonely coast.

Start: At 892437, the car park, Holkham.

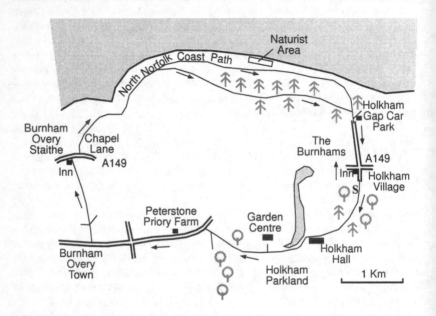

From the car park, turn right towards Holkham Hall. Go through the park gates and continue along a tarmac drive, passing **Bygones** and **Holkham Hall**, on your left. Continue with a lake on your right, following a drive around the western side of the hall. Turn right along a track signposted for the Garden Centre.

Pass the Garden Centre on your right and continue westwards along the drive. Leave Holkham Hall through the gates at West Lodge and, ignoring a footpath to the left, continue to reach a road. Turn left to pass Peterstone Priory Farm on your right, continuing to a crossroads. Go straight over and continue past the sign for Burnham Overy Town. Now, just before the first bungalow on your right, turn right along a track, going uphill between fields. At end of the field the track bends right and then left: continue uphill, northwards, ignoring footpaths to both right and left.

Follow the track over the crest of the hill to enter **Burnham Overy Staithe**. Go past the Hero Inn, and turn right, with care, along the main road (the A149). After about 100 yards, at the end of the wall and fence, cross the road into the very narrow Chapel Lane. At the end of the lane, turn left and then, after 5 yards, turn right up on to the seawall. Turn right and follow the Coastal Path along the seawall, with grazing marsh to your right and sea marsh to your left. After $1^1/_2$ miles the path peters out into sand dunes: follow the clear path eastwards, either on the sand (at low tide only!), or through the dunes.

After $3/_4$ mile, a belt of pines begins: about $1^1/_2$ miles after the start of the pines, turn right through the trees to reach the car park at Holkham Gap (the increasing density of beach visitors is a guide). Ice-cream is available here. Continue south along the drive/road to the A149. Cross, again with care, and continue ahead along the drive towards the Hall to regain the start.

POINTS OF INTEREST:

Bygones – This is a collection of memorabilia owned by Dick Joice. It is a collection of tools and machinery from farms, homes and agricultural industries connected with the area. There are also many steam organs and engines. A visit is a fascinating way to spend an afternoon.

Holkham Hall – The Hall is privately owned by the Earl of Leicester. It was built in the late 18th century by the first Earl. Building was a lengthy process as the Earl lost a fortune in the 'South Sea Bubble' scandal. Away to the north you can just see the top of the monument erected to the memory of Thomas Coke known as 'Coke of Norfolk'. He was responsible for many agricultural innovations including the four-course rotation of crops. Later he became the Father of the House of Commons. In 1837 Queen Victoria made him Earl Leicester of Holkham. The Hall is open to the public.

Please Note: All routes through the park are by permission only. Fallow deer are kept here so no dogs please.

Burnham Overy Staithe – This was the port serving all the Burnham villages. Sadly, silting of the harbour has restricted modern use to small boats. The Hero Inn commemorates Admiral Lord Nelson who was born and kept a home at Burnham Thorpe. As you watch the small boats here think back a few years for Nelson himself learnt his naval tricks in these waters. Close manoeuvring in shallow water was his forte.

REFRESHMENTS:

The Hero Inn, Burnham Overy Staithe. There are also tearooms at Bygones, and tearooms and an inn, *The Victoria*, at Holkham village.

Walk 95   SALTHOUSE AND CLEY   10m (16km)

Maps: OS Sheets Landranger 133; Pathfinder 820.

A gem of a coastal walk. One for twitchers.

Start: At 074439, Salthouse Green, adjacent to the Dun Cow Inn on the A149.

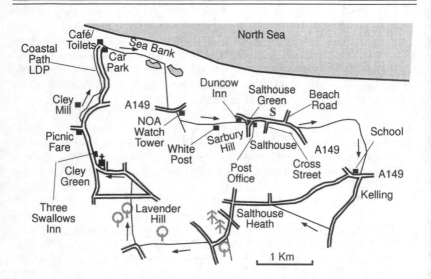

From the Green, go eastwards, with care, along the main road, passing the Post Office and shellfish shops on your right. Pass Cross Street, also on your right, and Beach Road, on your left, then, about 100 yards after the de-restriction sign, where the road bends sharp right, fork left along a track. Follow the track, eventually bending right to the A149 again. Cross, with care, and go uphill along the minor road opposite, signposted for Holt. Follow the road through Kelling and continue uphill to reach power lines at the top. There, turn right along a track which, later, becomes overgrown. Ignore all farm tracks off to both left and right, following the track to a road.

Turn left and, ignoring a road to the right, follow the road to a crossroads. Turn left and, at the next junction, go straight on along a road signposted for Holt. The road bends right, through trees, to reach a T-junction: cross and go straight ahead along the track opposite, following it for $^3/_4$ mile to reach the corner of a minor road. Turn right here, heading northwards along a footpath. Walk with a hedge on your right, then go through hedge gap and maintain direction, still with a hedge on your right. Follow the path through a thicket and up and over Lavender Hill. The path now descends to a road: cross and maintain direction along the footpath opposite to reach another road. Turn left and follow the road down into **Cley** village passing the church and the Three Swallows Inn on your right and Cley Green on your left. Ignore all minor roads off to both left and right to reach a T-junction by Picnicfare. Turn right and, opposite the telephone box, turn left up a path between cottages. At its end, turn right. You are now on the Norfolk Coastal Path – an official National Trail. Follow the Path, with houses on your right and passing Cley Mill on your left. Go up and down steps, then follow the clear path which, later, becomes a raised bank with a road and grazing marshes to your right.

At the Cley Beach Café, turn right and follow a path, walking with the sea bank on your left and a Reserve on your right. After $^3/_4$ mile, turn right at a waymarker on a wooden post and follow a raised path, with a fence/pond on your right, to reach the A149 again. Turn left, with care, and, after 100 yards, turn right at a NOA sign and follow a footpath signposted for **Salthouse** through a thicket. At the end of the thicket turn left along another path signposted for Salthouse, following it across a field. Continue eastwards with a hedge on your right to reach a white post. There, go through the hedge and follow a path across the field beyond to reach a stile. Cross on to Sarbury Hill and go up and over it on a path that reaches another stile. Cross into a field and follow the hedge on your left to a stile. Cross and follow the path beyond behind gardens. At its end, cross a stile to return to The Green.

POINTS OF INTEREST:
Cley – Pronounced Cly. This was an important wool port in the 16th century. The Mill is delightful and is open to the public. The very fortunate can stay as it is also a superior class Bed and Breakfast establishment.
Salthouse – The name is Saxon – meaning (unsurprisingly) 'a place for keeping salt'. Salt was extracted from seawater and was used for preserving fish. Salt was also exported to places as far away as Iceland in the 18th century.

REFRESHMENTS:
The Dun Cow, Salthouse.
The Three Swallows Inn, Cley Green.
The Cley Beach Café, a twitchers haunt, on the route.

Walk 96   SHOULDHAM WARREN   10m (16km)

Maps: OS Sheets Landranger 132 or 143; Pathfinder 880.

Forest, river bank and pasture.

Start: At 636134, the layby on the A10 just south-east of Setchey Bridge.

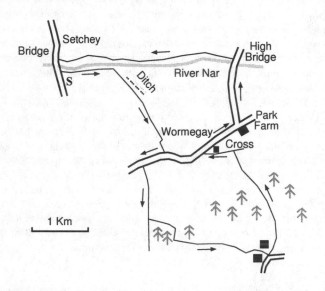

From the northern (bridge) end of the layby, take the path between brick walls (signed as part of the Nar Valley Way). Follow the brick wall around to the left to join the riverbank and turn right along it. Follow the path across two stiles. Then, after $^1/_2$ mile, and shortly after crossing a third stile, the path bears right, firstly with and then away from, the river. Here, where the bank goes left to rejoin the river, go straight ahead to reach a wooden bridge. Cross and continue along the top of the bank for about a mile. Go over a stile and, after a few yards, bear right, away from the bank, then left along a field edge, walking with a fence on the right. Cross a stile to join the road at Wormegay.

Turn right along a road to reach a housing estate on the left. Take the second road on the left (Craven Lane), following it past a road on the right, opposite a pond. After a further 200 yards, just after the start of a wood on the left, turn left along a signed footpath between fences. Go past a drainage ditch on the left, following the path to where it ends at a broad, crossing track. Turn right for 300 yards to reach a cross-tracks (there is a gate and 'Private' sign on the right here). Turn sharp left along the track, joining a track from the right and continuing ahead to meet another track on the right. Bear left with the main track, going over at the next cross-tracks, through a gate and ahead at another cross-tracks. The track bears sharp left, then right towards houses: continue ahead between the houses, bearing right with the track. After passing the first houses on the right, you reach a metalled road: bear right along it to reach a road and track junction. Turn sharp left between two **forest** signs, going along a narrow, earth path which runs parallel with a broad, sandy track on the right. At a track junction, go right, through a barrier, and turn left along the broad main track.

Continue uphill, following red and yellow, and then red, waymarker posts. Where the red markers turn left at a cross-tracks, continue straight ahead along a grey sandy track to reach a footbridge at the forest edge. Cross and continue uphill, passing a pond on the left to reach a track at a T-junction. Turn left to reach Wormegay village at the village sign.

Turn sharp right along the road and, after $^1/_2$ mile, turn left with the road at Park Farm and continue over a drainage ditch to reach a river bridge at power lines. Cross the bridge and turn left along a signed path along the riverbank for 2 miles to reach the road at Setchey Bridge. Turn left to return to the start.

POINTS OF INTEREST:

Forest – The forest is Shouldham Warren, part of Lynn Forest, the mostly westerly of the East Anglian forests. Most of the original broad-leaved trees planted have been replaced by conifers, but sections of the original forest still remain.

REFRESHMENTS:

None on the route, but available at Shouldham Village about a mile off route and on the A10 at Tottenhill, 2 miles south of Setchey.

Walk 97　RINGSTEAD AND HOLME-NEXT-THE-SEA　10m (16km)

Maps: OS Sheets Landranger 132; Pathfinder 818 and 839.

Unspoilt coastal scenery, a nature reserve and rolling farmland with good views.

Start: At 705406, Ringstead Church.

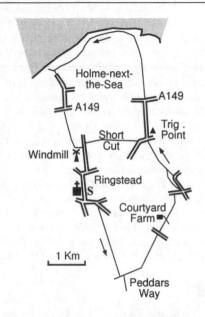

From the church, turn right, downhill, and at the road junction, follow the main road around to the left. At the next junction, turn right, then, where the road bears left, continue ahead along Peddars Way South, heading south along the Way, which soon becomes a sandy track. Continue ahead at a track junction and, at the next junction, after about 50 yards, go straight ahead along a narrow track. Follow the track to the left and the right, and then go through a gap to walk with a hedge on your left. On reaching a metalled track turn left and follow it to a road. Cross and continue along metalled road opposite (signposted for **Courtyard Farm**). Where the road turns left to the farm, continue ahead along a sandy track to reach a road.

Turn right, soon reaching a crossroads. Turn left and immediately left again through a hedge gap and bear right along the edge of the field beyond, as indicated by the arrowed footpath sign. At the end of the field, turn right through a gap and left along a broad track to reach a road near a trig. point. A short cut is possible from here, turning left to follow a track which runs due west to reach the Holme-Ringstead road close to the windmill.

Continue ahead along the road opposite – there are good sea views from here – to reach the main road (the A149). Cross, with care, and go along the track opposite. Go through a metal gate by a barn on to a grassy track and follow it to reach another metal gate. Turn left over a footbridge and then right to walk between a fence and a ditch. Bear left with the track then go right to cross another footbridge. Go across a field and, where the track bears left, cross a ditch and continue with the ditch on your left. On reaching an embankment, turn left through a gate on to the Coast Path through the **Holme Dunes Nature Reserve**.

Follow the track through a wood and, shortly after leaving the trees, ascend an embankment along a boardwalk. Now continue along the main track, ignoring a sign for a car park, to reach a track junction. Turn left towards a house. Go through a wooden gate – there are public toilets on the right – and continue ahead along a road, passing a road to Holme village on the left. At the main road (the A149 again) cross, again with care, and follow the narrow track opposite, just to the right of a drive, passing a garage on the left. Continue along a track between hedges and, at a cross hedge just before a windmill, follow the track around to the left to reach a road. The short cut track comes in just to the north of this point. Turn right along the road, going right at the first junction and left at the next to return to the start.

POINTS OF INTEREST:

Courtyard Farm – The farm is owned by a charitable trust administered by a well-known conservationist peer. It comprises 750 acres including five miles of newly created public footpaths providing three circular walks. A farm building has been converted to a bunkhouse barn providing basic accommodation.

Holme Dunes Nature Reserve – The Reserve covers an unspoilt coastal area of sand dunes providing a habitat for many rare plants, insects and birds.

REFRESHMENTS:

There are inns at both Ringstead and Holme, though the latter is about $\frac{1}{2}$ mile off the route. There is also a teashop at Ringstead and a refreshment bar at Holme beach, though this is generally open at weekends and in high season only.

Maps: OS Sheets Landranger 133; Pathfinder 820.

A splendid walk: north Norfolk at its finest.

Start: At 157432, the Pay and Display car park, Station Approach, Sheringham.

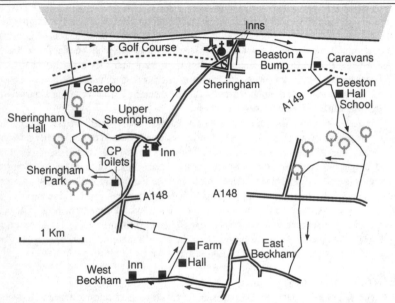

Head down Station Road and High Street to the sea front. At the promenade, turn right for 400 yards to reach the toilets. There, turn right up steep steps and keep ahead along a road. Turn left at a T-junction (signposted Peddars Way/Coastal Path) and follow a path up and over Beeston Bump. At the far side, just before a caravan site, turn right and follow a low bank on your left to Priory View and the railway. Cross the railway and continue up a drive to the A149. Cross, with care, and turn left into a layby. Go along a drive, passing cottages, Beeston Hall School and a farm on your left, then follow a wide track towards woodland. Turn left then, after 300 yards, turn right, going steeply uphill through trees.

At the top, in a clearing where five tracks meet, keep ahead through a barrier and, after 300 yards, turn right along a wide crossing track and follow as it winds through trees to the A148. Cross, with care, into the green lane opposite (signposted for Beckham), and follow it to its end. Now turn right along a gravel track to East Beckham village. Keep ahead along the road to a fork. Bear left (signposted for West Beckham), but 5 yards after the phonebox on your left, turn left up a drive/ footpath. Follow the path as it becomes a green lane, and at its end cross a road into the minor road opposite (signposted for West Beckham).

After 1,000 yards, turn right up a farm drive/footpath. Pass the farm on your right and, after a further 100 yards, at a path junction, turn left (look for the yellow arrow) and follow a path along the right edge of three fields to reach a road. This is not as on the OS Map - use the arrows as your guide. Turn right to reach the A148 again. Cross, with care, to the entrance to **Sheringham Park**. Follow the drive to a car park, exiting at its north-western corner along a footpath marked by a red/blue post. Follow the red marked path, initially going steeply downhill, then swinging right and uphill to reach a T-junction. Turn left.

At the next T-junction, a short cut, or detour, turns right, following a track to a road at Upper Sheringham. Walk ahead, passing the **church**. Now either reverse the route back to the T-junction, or follow the road, the B1157, back to Sheringham.

The main route turns left at the T-junction. Go through a gate and turn right (signposted Gazebo) and walk with a wood on your right to reach the A149. Cross, with care, into the field opposite, entering via a wood barrier, and turn right to reach a stile. Turn left along a green lane, following it to the cliff top. Turn right towards Sheringham. After passing a paddling pool on your right, turn right to a roundabout. Go straight on into Church Street, cross into St Peter's Road and continue to the North Norfolk Railway. Turn left to return to the start.

POINTS OF INTEREST:
Sheringham Park – The Park has a splendid display of azaleas and rhododendrons in May, but the house is not open to the public. The grounds were designed by Humphrey Repton who wrote 'I can with truth pronounce that Sheringham possesses more natural beauty and local advantages, than any place I have every seen'.
Upper Sheringham Church – The church has carved 15th-century pew ends – one depicting a mermaid in gratitude to the mermaid who slithered ashore to say a prayer for the souls of poor drowned fishermen.

REFRESHMENTS:
There is plenty of choice in Sheringham and an inn, *The Red Lion*, at Upper Sheringham.

Walk 99   AYLSHAM   11m (17¹/₂km)

Maps: OS Sheets Landranger 134, Pathfinder 861 and 862.
Easy tracks through farmland and by river.
Start: At 194268, the Burgh Road car park, Aylsham.

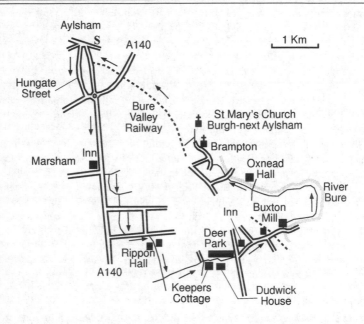

From the car park turn right, uphill, into the market square, **Aylsham**. Just before the Post Office, turn left into Hungate Street and walk to its end. Turn left into Orchard Lane and continue to the roundabout on the main road (the A140). Cross, with care, to the cycle way by the garden centre and restaurant and follow this downhill along an avenue of oaks to Marsham. About 100 yards after the Flag Inn, turn left along the track to Grove Farm. After 30 yards, turn right, uphill, between farm buildings. The track eventually becomes grassed: continue along it, ignoring a private track swinging away to the left to reach a minor road. Cross and carry on in same direction along the footpath opposite, beyond the barrier. At the path's end, turn left along a minor road to **Rippon Hall Farm** and turn right down the farm drive.

Follow the drive between farm buildings and, after $^1/_2$ mile, turn left (eastwards) along a wide track. After a further $^1/_2$ mile, ignore a track to the right, continuing to pass Keepers Cottage on your right. Bear left towards Dower House (away from the imposing Dudwick House) and follow a gravel track to reach park gates and a minor road. Cross and continue ahead (Crown Road) through the village of Buxton. At a junction bear right towards Coltishall, and at the next junction, by the village sign, turn left, following the road under a railway bridge. Now, as the road bends sharp right over the **River Bure** at a water mill, turn left up a signed brickweave drive. After 20 yards, bear right, away from some new houses, along a signed grassy path. The path passes in front of Riverside Cottage then swings right and left to reach the Bure's bank. Follow the bank for 2 miles, ignoring tracks off to the left and right to reach a minor road. Cross this and a narrow stile between two concrete blocks and continue along the river bank. After the second stile/fence, turn half-left across a field, aiming for a field gate by the cottages. Go through the gate and up a green lane (Common Lane) between cottages to reach a minor road. Turn right and follow the road as it bends sharp left, then right past Brampton Church.

At the end of the road, go ahead, through a farmyard, on to a concrete drive. Go downhill, through a gate and over a footbridge, turning left immediately to cross a second footbridge. It is worth a small diversion here to view St Mary's Church at Burgh next Aylsham.

To continue, follow the right bank of the stream, then the left bank (crossing via an earth bridge) to reach a railway bridge. Few walks give you the opportunity to meet a Mermaid - this stream is The Mermaid. At the bridge, turn left, up steps, to reach the Bure Valley Railway path. Turn right and follow the path for 2 miles to **Aylsham** station. From the station car park, turn right along Norwich Road, then right again down Burgh Road to return to the car park.

POINTS OF INTEREST:

River Bure – The section of the walk from Buxton to Brampton follows 'the lap, lap, lapping of the weedy Bure' to use the words of Sir John Betjeman.

Aylsham – This interesting market town was the main town of John of Gaunt's Duchy in Norfolk in the 14th century - hence the town sign.

Rippon Hall Farm – The white cattle with black ears and noses seen here are British Whites.

REFRESHMENTS:

There are opportunities at Aylsham, Buxton and Marsham.

Walk 100 BURGH CASTLE AND BELTON 11m (17½km)

Maps: OS Sheets Landranger 134; Pathfinder 904.

A walk of wild marshes, ancient history and modern recreation.

Start: At 520081, the British Rail Station, Great Yarmouth.

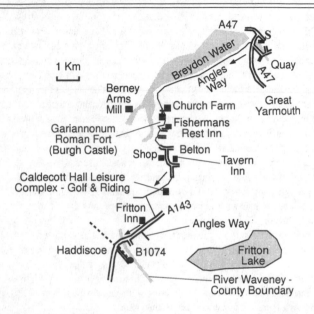

NOTE: This walk is linear, connecting two rail station. The two are not on the same line, a change being necessary at the intervening Reedham. A practical solution is to park at Reedham or Norwich stations, take the short train ride to Yarmouth's Vauxhall Station to start, and then to do a one train hop at the finish.

From the station car park – the station is signed from the A47, or you can look for the ASDA supermarket! – head south-eastwards and cross an old bridge by Weavers Way/**Angles Way** information boards. Turn left towards the main road, going along the Quay. Turn right towards the ships, then right again over South Town Bridge. Now, after the Rocket Inn, turn right yet again along Mill Lane. At its end, continue ahead along a path to a road, continuing along the road. Turn right just after a playground to reach the riverbank and turn left to follow a clear path under the A47.

Follow the path for 3 miles, with Breydon Water on your right, to where the path (and the water) turns south. Now, after a further $^1/_2$ mile, turn left, away from the water, going uphill along a footpath to reach Burgh Church. Go past the church, on your right, then turn right along a gravel track to **Burgh Castle**. At the far end of the site (where the gravel track also ends), turn right to return to the riverbank and turn left along it.

Just after the Fisherman's Rest, turn left, uphill, along a driveway, passing a boatyard entrance and then turning right through a red and white barrier. Follow the footpath beyond, walking with a fence on your right and eventually returning to the river. After about 200 yards, turn left over a stile and follow the clear, waymarked, path beyond across a field to reach a lane by some houses. Pass the houses on your right, follow the lane as it bends left and uphill into Belton. Turn right along Station Road North, passing a shop on your right. Now, opposite The Tavern, turn right along Sandy Lane and, at its end, carry straight on along a sandy track, going through the Caldecott Hall complex. After $^1/_2$ mile, just before a house on the left, turn left along a clear, waymarked, path heading south-eastwards, following the hedge on your right at first, and then the hedge on your left. The path enters a green lane: continue along this to reach the main road (the A143). Turn right, with care, and follow the road through the pretty village of Fritton (the village inn is on your right). Ignore Angles Way, which is signposted off to the left, and the B1074 to St Olaves, which also goes off to the left, staying on the main road to cross two bridges into Suffolk. At the far end of second bridge, turn left to Haddiscoe Station.

POINTS OF INTEREST:
Angles Way – Much of this route follows this walk, a 77-mile stroll linking the Broads and Weavers Way with the Brecks and Peddars Way/Icknield Way. It meanders through the Waveney Valley area marking the border between Norfolk and Suffolk. The route was developed by the Ramblers Association of both counties together with the Councils. Thanks to all concerned, the waymarking is good, mostly yellow discs with an otter motif.
Burgh Castle – The walls you see are the remains of a Norman castle built on top of a Roman fort. In Roman times Breydon Water was much wider, its extent marked by the positions of Burgh Castle and Caister Castle on the opposite shore. This spot was home to the Dalmatian Cavalry.

REFRESHMENTS:
There is plenty of choice in Yarmouth, Belton and Fritton, including those inns mentioned in the route description.

TITLES IN THE SERIES